THE WOODS AFIRE

THE MEMOIRS OF A GEORGIA TEACHER BEFORE AND AFTER DESEGREGATION

Ruth B. Crawford

THE WOODS AFIRE

THE MEMOIRS OF A GEORGIA TEACHER BEFORE AND AFTER DESEGREGATION

by Ruth Burton Crawford

Regent Press
1996

Copyright ©1992 by Ruth Burton Crawford.

Library of Congress Cataloging-in-Publication Data

Crawford, Ruth Burton, 1917-
   The woods afire : the memories of a Georgia teacher before and after desegregation / by Ruth Burton Crawford.
      p.   cm.
      ISBN 0-916147-98-3
   1. Crawford, Ruth Burton, 1917- . 2. Afro-American teachers--Georgia--Biography. 3. Afro-American women--Georgia--Biography. 4. School integration--Georgia--History. I. Title. LA2317.C74A3   1996
371.1'0092--dc20
[B]
                                                              96-26366
                                                                   CIP

Manufactured in the United States of America
Regent Press
6020-A Adeline Street
Oakland, CA 94608

Table of Contents

Introduction		*i*
Acknowledgments		*iii*
Dedication		*v*
Chapter 1	Georgia Roots	*1*
Chapter 2	Painful Experience	*7*
Chapter 3	Near Thing	*15*
Chapter 4	Easter Finery	*23*
Chapter 5	Sweet Times	*29*
Chapter 6	High School Days	*35*
Chapter 7	Off to Augusta	*43*
Chapter 8	Racial Matters	*53*
Chapter 9	Paine College Days	*61*
Chapter 10	Teacher At Last	*69*
Chapter 11	Coming of Age	*77*
Chapter 12	A Rewarding Year	*85*
Chapter 13	A Dishonored Student	*91*
Chapter 14	The Good War	*99*
Chapter 15	Marriage and Motherhood	*105*
Chapter 16	New School Ventures	*113*
Chapter 17	Graduate School	*123*
Chapter 18	Integration	*129*
Chapter 19	Black and White	*135*
Chapter 20	The Augusta Riot	*143*
Chapter 21	Final Days	*151*
Chapter 22	Closing the Books	*159*

Introduction

I wrote this book with the hope that it might reach people who have a problem about why they hate others—particularly people of color. I want the reader to understand that the lynching of blacks was horrifying, but most white people never participated in such an event, and many sought to do the right thing, during and after segregation.

You might say the truly bad ones were like poor folks in that they just kept multiplying. Yet, we know we must live and work together, or else we will destroy each other. My many life experiences and years of teaching prepared me to make my contributions to humanity while contending with both good and bad people. Early on, fortunately, I learned that the melodious music of the piano results from the interaction of black and white keys.

I have lived through segregation in what was one of the most segregated states in the nation: discrimination of every type, share-cropping, hard times, and war years. However, I have never learned to hate. Indeed, the love and generosity of family and Christian teachings make me pity the hate-monger. Sadly, hate eats insidiously at the very heart of people. I was hurt on many occasions by such people, but I believe their hate only cost them the loss of their souls.

To this day, decades after her death, I can still hear my mother saying, "If you hate me because I'm dirty, I'll go wash. If you hate me because I'm ignorant, I'll get an education. If you hate me because I'm black, you ll have to talk to God about that."

What I am today is based on the experiences I have recorded in the past 75 years. Out of those experiences, I have garnered the friendship of people of all races, colors, and creeds. I think of them like the hair on my head, a thick intertwining of black and white.

I am reminded of a small child's comments when integration began and a black family moved into a white neighborhood. The child told her mother that she wished the black family had more than one child or that additional black families would move into the neighborhood.

"You see, Mother, I'll have to like the one black child whether she's good or bad. If I don't, they'll say I'm prejudiced. If there were several black girls, I would have a choice then to pick one as my friend."

Then there was the white college president who was walking along the street with two black students when a gang of white boys confronted them, saying, "We don't get out of the way for niggers and dogs."

Without raising his voice, the white president informed his students, "We do, so we'll just walk around these young men."

Combating racism is a never ending task. For every hard won victory, there is a cruel defeat. Yet, I believe that in resisting racism, we grew stronger, more confident, and better citizens.

In telling the story of my life from World War I to the present and my 37 years as a teacher, I hope to provide the reader with valuable and helpful anecdotes that they might possibly use to smooth their path through the intricacies of human relations.

In closing, I have never lost my love of teaching and still teach in every way possible. Although I have been retired from formal teaching for 17 years, I use such experiences to assist others. I still believe in teaching as if the woods were on fire.

Acknowledgements

I want to give special thanks to my editor, James W. Ryan, a veteran Boston writer and historian, who saw the possibilities in my fledgling manuscript and agreed to work with me to fashion it into a book.

My gratitude is also extended to the Layman family of the Boston suburb of Arlington for their hospitality and advice regarding the manuscript. My sister, Costella Layman, was especially helpful in reading the manuscript and suggesting further ideas to enhance it. I should mention that it was at her home that I first met Mr. Ryan and had the opportunity to discuss the manuscript's potential with him for about four hours.

Much credit must also go to my grandson, George I. Crawford, Jr. of Aiken, South Carolina, who researched old newspapers and microfilm files for the necessary background material, and to my grandson, Marcus Crawford, who took me on a tour of my old hometown, the town of Nuberg, Georgia.

My niece, Monique Mattison designed the cover for *Woods Afire*. The structure shown is made of an interior frame system which is resistant to flames but has a completely superficial system of walls which appear to burn away exposing the teacher and students inside. The idea is that the flames of prejudice and hatred may cause harm on the surface but the heart and strength of the structure (the frame) has never been affected and will forever endure.

Finally, I would be remiss if I were not to express my heartfelt appreciation to my Shiloh Community Center assistant, Sherrie Hill, who listened patiently to my recollections and typed the manuscript from my scribbled notes. Similar thanks go to Miss Willie Mae Jordan, the librarian at Paine College, who provided historical materials and encouraged me to complete the manuscript.

This picture depicts a marker showing Elbert County, Georgia, the Granite Capital of the World, and Ruth B. Crawford, with her grandson, Marcus. The birthplace of the author is Nuberg, a little hamlet between Elbert County and Hart County, Georgia.

Dedication

This book is dedicated to my beloved family: George Isaac Crawford, my son, who always wanted me to be happy and to pursue my dream. Delores Ann Crawford, my daughter-in-law, who always provided love and encouragement. My grandchildren—Christine, George I., and Marcus—to whom I leave this book as part of my legacy.

Very importantly, my family also includes my sisters—Lois Carter and Costella Layman—and my brother, Nathaniel Hawthorne Burton, all of whom provided material for this work just by being members of the family.

Then, of course, I must mention my parents, Lizzie and Jacob Burton, who taught me to love mankind and instilled in me a deep and abiding belief and love in Jesus Christ.

The Crawford Family:
Seated: Marcus, grandson of the author. Standing (from left to right): George I. Crawford, son of the author; daughter-in-law Delores; granddaughter, Christine; the author, and grandson, George, Jr.

Chapter 1

Georgia Roots

WHEN I WAS OLD ENOUGH and I could understand, mama told me I was born when Mr. Woodrow Wilson was president in the last year of the war. She said how he was a Southerner, too, a white gentleman who had taught at some college in the North before going to the White House. He had not wanted to get America into the World War, she recalled, but the Germans said they were going to sink all our ships without a warning, and Mr. Wilson thought it was time to stand up to them.

Anyway, I was born in a little hamlet called Nuberg. It wasn't much bigger than a flyspeck on a map. It's in Hart County way up in the northeast corner of Georgia, across the Savannah River from South Carolina. These 75 years later, Nuberg still isn't much more than a whistle stop between two black churches at Norman's Grove and Flat Rock. It wouldn't even have been a hamlet back then without the country store which sold everything except clothing. Strange, huh? You wanted clothing. You had to go up to Hartwell, which liked to pretend it was a real big town.

My mama and papa were Lizzie and Jacob Burden. Mama was an Oglesby. Pa was a hardworking, sharecropper farmer on a plantation owned by a white man named Allen Thornton. My papa married my mama when he was about 25 and she was 14. He said he had to marry her young because she was the prettiest girl in the Maple Spring Church, and he didn't want anybody else to take her away.

My father only knew that his mother was Caroline Jacob Burden, who was born in 1826 and died in January, 1911, and other than that neither he nor my mother knew much of anything about their family histories. They had no recollections about their origins, about any of their people, or about when their folks came to this country. It wasn't hard to understand when I remember how hard they had to work to feed and clothe 14 children in some very trying times.

Years later, they would change the family name to Burton because my third oldest sister Carrie didn't want

The tombstone of Caroline Burden, grandmother of Ruth Burton Crawford. This is the Church cemetery where Caroline Burden was buried in 1911, 84 years ago.

Note: The name BURDEN was changed to BURTON when the older sister, Carrie, went to college.

anyone to get the idea that we would be a burden to society in any way. Carrie was a graduate of Paine College and loved to play with words and she decided on the new spelling for the name.

Nearby, there was a big white house owned by the local white doctor, Joe Harper. He had a big yard, and the patients stood around under the trees—especially black women—waiting to see him. Dr. Harper delivered white babies sometimes. Never black babies, though. Black midwives delivered black babies. I remember that he was a very kind man. Mrs. Harper was not so kind.

My sister-in-law Pearlie Burton, who was married to my brother, Fayette, also known as "Fate" and "Red" because of his coloring, was the midwife for most of the black women in Hart and Elbert Counties. I remember that Pearlie would lug around her big midwife satchel that was stuffed with clean white towels, rolls of bandages, scissors and jars of herbs. Many times I'd see her taking everything out of the bag to sterilize them on the stove.

Lots of new mothers didn't have any money and would pay Pearlie with foods like peas and peanuts and other farm grown products. Many of the young girls who had babies with light coloring would claim Red was the father and she wouldn't charge them. Since she had no children of her own, she'd accept the babies of unmarried girls who also said Red was the pappa. In time, she had eight children who loved her dearly.

My mama told me that when she became pregnant with me, a white woman—Mrs. Janie Warren, whose family had a dairy farm—said how much she admired her for having a 13th child. Mrs. Janie asked Mama whether she would name me after her. It was supposed to be good luck of some sort. My mother had already picked out the name Ruth from the Bible for me, but as a compromise she gave me the name Janie Ruth.

However, when I was born, the name Janie Ruth

seemed to fit me. I often wondered, though, how they knew the baby in my mother's womb was going to be a girl. There were no tests in those days to determine the sex of the unborn child. Mama said womenfolk had their own ways and signs to learn such things. In later years, I heard mama say that any pregnant woman who stepped off first on her right foot was sure to have a girl.

No matter, I was born a girl, a beautiful one, I was always told. My actual birthday, however, has always remained a mystery. I thought for a while it was May 25, 1917. Then I found a census report much later, dated January 20, 1917, which stated that I was four-and-a-half-months-old on that date. That being so, I figured I was born in the first week of September, 1918, about two months before the end of the war. You have to remember that in those days, midwives sometimes didn't get to the county seat in Hartwell for months, if ever, to report black births out in the countryside. They had neither a horse nor automobile to get them there.

Since I was the 13th child, mama and papa thought I would be the last one. My mother was about 40 then, and father was 50. Believing that, they made a big fuss over me and showed me off every chance. Mama always said I was a beautiful baby. There are baby pictures of me, but none of the previous 12 babies. I was "It" like that old movie star, Clara Bow, or whoever.

But life is full of surprises, sometimes happy, and along came another girl, whom they named Costella. She tells me that I am still the baby, and she is the youngest child in the family. All these years later, we are still the best of friends as well as sisters even though for years now she's been living way up north in the town of Arlington outside of Boston.

All 14 of us children were born at home in Nuberg, delivered by midwives. In those days, we lived in a large one-story wooden house on the Thornton land. It had a whole bunch of bedrooms and a big kitchen and a porch that ran all the way around the house and was a great place to play on rainy days. There was a pump for the water, outhouses for nature's calls, and a ramshackled barn for our few farm animals—particularly for our great old horse, Dan. As far as I know, then and now, the Burton family has always owned land somewhere or other in Georgia.

This picture shows the pump for the water, the outhouse, and the side of the house similar to where the 14 Burton children lived with their parents.

The house sat snugly on a rolling hill, and down below, there was a creek that you crossed to gain a path through the woods. Georgia land is good land—hot land. Best for growing crops like cotton, peaches, peanuts, and tobacco. In those days, the woods held a variety of trees, including poplar and gum, elegant white and yellow pines, and Johnson and Bermuda grass. Wildlife still abounded then in the form of rabbits and raccoons, foxes and possums. The air was redolent with the smells of wild flowers and pine pitch and riven with the calls of myriad birds: the blue jay, cardinal, mockingbird, owls, and Georgia's official bird, the brown thrasher. Danger lurked in the red clay soil in the shapes of rattlesnakes and water moccasins.

One day my brother, "N.H.", and I were walking along

the creek when a lengthy coach whip snake crossed our path. I jumped a mile but quick as a wink N.H. swung his shovel at that snake and took its head clean off. The snake whipped away, leaving its head behind. I reminded N.H. that the snake would only die when the sun went down. We got out of there fast.

Picture of the highway leading in to Nuberg, Georgia, the birthplace of Ruth B. Crawford.

Chapter 2

Painful Experience

I WASN'T MUCH HIGHER THAN OUR BIG OLD DOG when I was taught to help in the kitchen. My favorite chore was to lend a hand with the cooking. I also thought it was great fun to sift the flour for the biscuits mama made fresh every day for papa. Many a time, I got the flour all over my face and clothes.

When I was a little older, I got to help mama and the other kids chase after the chickens out in the yard. Gosh, could they run! It was nothing to take half an hour to catch one or two chickens. Then we'd put them in a special coop to clean them out since they thought nothing of eating anybody's droppings.

One of the preachers, Rev. J. E. Murray, from the Colored Methodist Episcopal Church was forever eating at our house on Sunday because he said, "Sister Lizzie was bound to clean out her chickens." He knew she did, he'd say, because he could tell by the taste of the chicken. I noticed, though, that he always watched my mother when she went out to get a fresh chicken out of the coop.

I can still see my mother ringing the chicken's neck, whirling it around until the neck snapped, and the head flew off. No matter, the chicken would still flutter for a while when she laid it on the ground to die. The chicken then would be soaked in boiling water, removed and plucked, cut up, salted and floured, and placed in steaming hot grease and cooked until it was crisp and brown. It was beautiful and delicious.

It was always served to the preachers first, and they'd take all the good meaty parts while we children watched with our tongues hanging out. The preachers even took all the giblet gravy and poured it over their rice serving. In the end, we got to eat only the bony parts of the poor chicken.

Well, one of my older sisters got tired of waiting on the preachers to eat and asked mama to let her make the gravy. She really made good brown gravy—gravy that always smelled delicious. She kept taste-testing the gravy and eating the giblets as she prepared it. Finally, only a chicken head was left in the gravy, and she took it off the stove to serve to the preachers.

Reverend Nunally—or maybe it was Reverend Murray—took up a big spoon to ladle himself out some gravy on his rice and swirled the spoon about in vain to find some giblets. All he could bring up was the chicken head. He turned to mama and said, "Sister Lizzie, I guess this just must be the Big Head Gravy."

All of us giggled, but my sister who had eaten the giblets burst into laughter and had to leave the table.

With the warm sultry weather, flies were always a problem when food was set out on the table—especially since the house had no screens on the doors and windows. To keep them away, papa made himself a homemade fan out of a wooden cross to which he attached strips of newspapers. The fan was dangled from the ceiling over the table and strings ran from it to a pedal on the floor. Each meal, one of us kids was assigned to press the pedal and keep the fan shooing away the flies. When company was coming, two of us would dress up and stand at each end of the table and fan the air with more newspapers as an added measure to keep away the flies.

One of my earliest memories is that of mama getting us up and fed and dressed and rushing us off to school. We went down the hill and across the creek and along the path through the woods to the school house. It seemed like the sun always was just coming up when we'd start out to walk. There were no school busses in those days.

I first went to a two-room school for first grade. Actually, it was one big room divided by a partition. I then went to a three-room school for the next three grades. The latter school was a Rosenwald School.

This is the three-room Rosenwald school that Ruth Burton Crawford attended in Nuberg, Georgia, in the second and third grades.

Mama told me later that Julius Rosenwald was a president at one time of Sears Roebuck & Company and that he made a large fortune. He was a very kind man and gave away a lot of his money to Negro schools and Jewish charities. Mama said he contributed enough money to build numerous small wooden school houses in the South for colored folks, beginning in the 1920s and up to 1948. Our own

Flat Rock Elementary School was built with his money.

All the students, of course, were black. The white kids went to their own public schools. All my teachers through elementary school were black. My very first teachers were my oldest sister, Pearl, and her husband, Sam Harper, who was also the school principal. She only died a little while ago at age 100. Sister or not, she was not easy on me. None of my sisters were ever easy on me. You got the devil from your sisters in school and got it again at home from mama and papa who heard the story.

I didn't have a white teacher until I went to the high school at Paine College in Augusta, down in Richmond County. There the faculty was black and white. That's the way the school originally was set up back in the 19th century. Something you didn't find anywhere else in Georgia then.

Anyway, we all went to the Flat Rock school for our first reading, writing, and arithmetic lessons. I believe I entered the first grade there in 1924. Mama says those days were known as the Jazz Age, and Mr. Harding and Mr. Coolidge were in the White House.

I never thought for a moment, when entering the first grade that some day I'd graduate from Paine College in Augusta and graduate school at Indiana University, and teach for almost four decades, and win all kinds of awards for it. I never imagined how important teaching would be in my life and how I would come to develop the philosophy of teaching as if the woods were on fire. When you're six, you think you're never going to be ten, never mind be old enough and educated enough to teach other kids.

Mama was not only insistent that we all get a good education, she was also very protective of us. I learned later that one of the main reasons she had us leave for school so early was to avoid the white kids. The Harper family were our neighbors, but we were never allowed to play outdoors when their kids were outside. Sometimes, though, she'd let my brothers play with them, but never us, girls.

It wasn't that we ever got into trouble with the white kids. It was just mother's way of trying to avoid that possibility. There were two worlds—the white world and the black one—and we seldom crossed over into the other one. That way, everybody got along even though we knew the whites didn't really like us. Mostly, we'd just do our work for them, whatever, and then go our separate ways.

I knew from early on there was a difference between us but didn't really become aware of it until I was about ten. I was at the Warren dairy farm of the woman whom I was named after—to help with the milking, only she didn't know I was around. She yelled at one of her boys who had done something wrong, "You're acting just like a "nigger." I don't think she had any idea I was about and came right out and said it.

Now, I was shocked and hurt because I had always thought of the Warren family as the grandest people in the world. Being young, I never thought color made a difference. It's just been black and white all your life. And there she was saying that word which is something you've known forever that you never want to hear. It's a slap in the face to call any black person a "nigger." That word is just taboo, and there was Miss Warren saying it.

Before that day, I'd never heard anyone use that word. No white person, in truth, had ever been unkind to me or called me any names. No, indeed. Probably because I'd been taught by mama and papa to be responsible for my own actions and my own character and not go blaming other people for my faults and weaknesses. I was taught, "You take care of yourself" and don't expect too much from other people—black or white.

Even though we lived on a big sharecrop farm with a whole lot of chores for all of us, mama saw to it that we went to school for the entire term. Other kids were kept at home to help out during the planting and harvesting seasons. But mama let Mr. Thornton know in no uncertain words that if we harvested our crops on time, her children would go to school.

To make sure it happened, we were up before the sun to work for a few hours and out into the fields until after sunset when we got home from school. On Saturdays, we worked from sunup to sunset to get our chores done. If all went well, we got a bonus in the form of a free Saturday afternoon to go into town, but that bonus was only available between the planting and harvesting times.

In truth, I liked the harvesting season. I thought it was fun to be so involved in bringing in the crops. I think I was about eight when mama said I could help pick the cotton. I was up before six o'clock to help fix breakfast and get the folks off to the fields. I think it was then that I began to become a leader because I would lead the pack many times in getting to the fields and in picking the cotton.

With my big old straw hat firmly fastened to my head, I'd put on my knee pads, take one of my three croker sacks, and get down on my knees and begin picking. For hours and hours, I'd crawl and pick, crawl and pick with the sun burning up the sky. As soon as I filled one sack, I'd drop it and begin filling a fresh one. When I had stuffed about five of them, I'd walk to the central pile and empty them out. When I was older, I'd sometimes average 200 pounds of cotton daily.

To me, there was nothing more beautiful during that time than to watch the pile of cotton grow into a mythical cotton candy mountain. Then the trucks would haul it away to the cotton gins down by a river or stream which was needed for power and there the seeds would be separated from the cotton balls. The seeds would be used later for meal and oil while the cotton was bound into 1,000-pound bales. The farmers would take the bales home until a buyer was found. Now and then we'd sell a bale for some special need.

One time, mama had fixed our lunch pails with fresh

Painful Experience

A field of cotton in Elbert County, Georgia, ready to be harvested. Ruth Burton Crawford is shown in the field.

biscuits, smeared with butter and syrup, and rushed us off to school. While we were gone, a white landowner sent his driver and truck to our house to pick us up to help pick cotton for him.

Seems Mr. Thornton had told him that we'd help him out. But mama told the driver that Mr. Thornton had no children in her house. If he was talking about her children, she said she'd decide how they would spend the day. From hearing stories like that, I learned early to stand on my own two feet.

Mama never failed to speak her mind. I remember now and then a white person would address her as "Auntie Lizzie." She'd waste not a moment to correct them. "My sisters ain't got no children who look anything like you," she'd tell them. She'd say, "They can inspect me if they want, but they will respect me, too."

Whenever there's a rumpus about my color, it makes no difference to me whether I'm liked or not as long as I'm respected. No matter what else, I demand respect.

I remember one time asking the United Way for a financial donation to assist my operation of the Shiloh Center. The white director jokingly responded that "it's Christmas, so give Ruth a turkey."

Looking him square in the eye, I said, "Mr. Joe, I don't need a turkey. What I need is some money to hire someone to cook the turkey."

Did he ever turn red! I just smiled innocently and went on to explain the facts of life in the black community.

Chapter 3

A Near Thing

YOU HAVE TO REMEMBER that when I was growing up that blacks—they called us colored or Negroes in that era—really weren't treated any better than in the days after the Civil War. Schools were tightly segregated all the way through college. The "equal but separate" doctrine was in full force.

Of course, our education was nowhere equal to that of the whites whether it was the quality of the teachers, the curriculum, or the buildings.

In many ways, black teachers had to be superstars. You see, we never got new books. Instead, the school officials would take the old books from the white schools, truck them to the black ones, and dump them in the school yard. Each teacher then had to pick through the pile to select the books needed for her classes—if they even were there. Oftentimes, you had to go by the size of the printed text to try and make a selection.

The desks and cabinets that were dumped in the yard likely as not had never been scrubbed. Many had layers of chewing gum attached to them. Also, on numerous occasions, they'd have notes attached to them with such comments as "Send this desk to the 'nigger' school." How unkind and humiliating!

Well, we often got lemons, and as a result, I informed my students that all you had to do was add enough water and sugar, and you got lemonade. In essence, I taught my black children that there was a positive side to anything if you looked for it. The key thing for them was to get a job and do it better than anyone else in order to keep it.

As I write this manuscript, I constantly see the results of my efforts to teach as if the woods were on fire. In the *Augusta Journal* (just today), I saw a photo and story about Classie Joe West, the aunt of movie star Lawrence Fishbourne, who had been named Teacher of the Year hereabouts. Classie was one of my students, and I must say she literally pulled herself up "by a string" because her family was so poor she couldn't afford the proverbial bootstrap.

No doubt that Classie, despite her childhood in poverty, became a great teacher. Somewhat modestly, she had even told me that she thinks she was taught well. I say, though, that she was taught better than that. She was taught as if the woods were on fire.

Another one of my students who went on to do well in the outside world is Eva Clayton, a native of Augusta, who now is the U.S. congresswoman from the First North Carolina District. Eva was in Augusta just this past April (1994) to speak at a fundraiser for my Shiloh Community Center. I must say that I considered her speech a masterpiece for a great cause.

One of my students who is in charge of maintenance supervision at a big mall often stops by to see me. He has arranged for the mall to give the pennies from the Wishing Well to help support Shiloh Comprehensive Community Center. You see, Shiloh is a non-profit organization that I started in 1978. Boy! You should see him in his uniform as he proudly steps into my office to greet his Teacher. He insists that I come to his Boss' office so she can talk with me and he can boastfully sing my praise. He often writes articles for the local newspapers. A former student of this caliber, epitomizes my philosophy of teaching as if the woods were on fire. I taught that one must get an honest job and do his best. How proud I am of my many students who are really carrying out my commitment! I see a little bit of me in everyone as they greet me.

Even today, as I walked into the library, I heard a voice call out, "Mrs. Crawford, do you remember me? I am Brenda; you taught me in 4th grade. I haven't seen you in 27 years." She was eager to help me find materials. She is one of the Historians at the main branch of the Library here in Augusta.

Looking at my teaching career, I am reminded of the giant ocean liner steaming out to sea. First though, the liner has to get out of the harbor, and I see myself as the little tugboat that pushes it into deep water and waits to return it safely to its berth.

I'm genuinely convinced today that my students love me for the caring way I took to teach them through so many years. Inevitably, I taught them as if the woods were on fire.

In that time too, blacks couldn't ride up front in public transportation and couldn't eat in the same restaurants with whites. Blacks also couldn't vote and work in certain jobs. Believe me, my people hated this system and retaliated in numerous but silent ways.

Old Gene Talmadge, who was a Phi Beta Kappa graduate of the University of Georgia, and a lawyer fiercely opposed blacks, unions, and communism, was riding high in the saddle in those days. He posed as the friend of the farmer and working man a modern day Robin Hood looking out for the poor.

In public, he was a vitriolic foe of blacks although in private he always treated them fairly. You see, in Georgia then, it was good politics to show a mean face to blacks.

No, Talmadge wasn't quite the man folks said. Talmadge knew deep down that the only way to get ahead, to get elected in Georgia, was to holler, "Nigger!" "Nigger!," every time he wanted to scare the poor whites. Still, he had black people on his farm whom he treated better than most people who supposedly thought like him.

Old Gene's supporters were mostly poor white farmers and laborers as well as the rich and powerful who were eager to maintain the status quo. Uneducated whites feared that blacks would put them out of work and rape their women. Along with Talmadge, they were staunch defenders of white supremacy.

Now his son, Herman—he was something else. I had heard he was hard on blacks, and I believed it because later in life I met him. I think he was just born mean and couldn't help himself, but I'll always remember that he was the governor who got teachers their first pay raise in years—black and white.

About the time the stock market crashed in 1929, my family had a trying time because of our color. My brother Nathaniel Hawthorne—we always called him "N.H."—was going to school alone, and he met a white girl named Sarah Sealy. Noticing that she was crying, he was prompted to ask her what the trouble was, but he remembered what his mama had taught him: "Never speak to white girls! Never. No good will come of it." With that admonition recalled, N.H. crossed to the other side of the road and went on to school.

The Sealy girl, meanwhile, proceeded sniffling and snuffling, to her own white school. We heard later that her teacher didn't ask why she was crying but inquired instead whether she had seen anyone on the way to school. She said that she had seen my brother. The local sheriff was informed, and he went to the black school and took my brother to the jail.

Mama and papa became frantic when informed about

N.H.'s arrest, but were warned to stay away from town because there already was talk of a lynching by an angry mob forming outside the jail. It was nothing in those days for the whites to lynch blacks—sometimes for hardly any reason at all.

Ironically, white men often had sex with black women and it was not unusual for pregnancies to occur, resulting in some white men having both a white and black family. Such things were never talked about openly but were well known in the two different worlds. The big majority of black men would not have anything to do with black women who had been with white men.

The county's white judge heard of the matter and hurried to the town square to tell the white mob that he would interrogate the girl and find out exactly what happened. He assured them that the guilty party would be found out before sunset that very day. He also noted that he had known my family for years and always found us to be respectable and law-abiding Negroes.

While the hours ticked by, we held fast to our house and were comforted by neighbors and friends who came by after hearing about N.H. When the preacher showed up, he led us in prayers for N.H.'s deliverance. Mama and papa were red-eyed but remained pillars of strength in our adversity. They held the judge to be an honest and fair man and believed wholeheartedly that he would do the right thing. Still, they were ever mindful of the many lynchings of blacks constantly occurring in the South then.

True to his word, the judge appeared before the mob before the sun went down. He reported that an examination had revealed that the Sealy girl had been badly whipped with a man's belt. She adamantly denied, however, that my brother had hurt her and finally admitted that her father had whipped her with his belt, warning her that he would kill her if she told anyone. She further admitted that, just like N.H. had said, my brother had never uttered a word to her and walked across to the opposite side of the road.

Of course, we were all overcome with joyful emotion and thanks-be-to-God on hearing of N.H.'s release and welcomed him home with a flood of tears, kisses, and prayers. In the days that followed, mama continued to warn us about how and when we should have contacts with whites.

A God-fearing woman, I never heard her utter any curses on Mr. Sealy's head, but I do remember when he died she wanted to know whether his remains had been placed in a vault and whether the vault had been tightly sealed. "I hope so," she added, "I want him to stay there forever."

My father just grinned and offered, "I know he will."

I guess you might say that was a time for hate and a time for love. The hate was evident in the mob who milled about outside of the jail and constantly shouted, "Lynch him! Lynch him!" But there was no hate in that lone Sealy girl who told the truth despite the fear of her father's threats.

As a child, I grew up with the knowledge that I lived in a segregated world. That awareness posed no problem for me because I was taught to be what I wanted to be. We were never taught that whites were superior to us, but we were also never taught that whites were a bunch of lynchers who hated us. No, we were taught that if you hated ignorance, get an education; if you hated dirt, take a bath; but if you were hated for being a black, then let the hater talk to God about that.

Later, when I went to Paine College, I learned about the college's founding fathers, Bishop W. R. Lambath and John Wesley Gilbert, who believed that whites and blacks could and should work together at their Christian co-educational college. The bishop was white, and Mr. Gilbert was black. My first experience there with segregation was at a football game where the white spectators were on one side of the field and the blacks on the other. When a few blacks went over to the white area, a big white man called the police and told him to get the blacks back to their side of the field.

Some students informed Paine's President, E. C. Peters, about the situation, and he noted that the college was founded by blacks and whites and would never practice anything differently than integration with the two races working in harmony. Still, the police were insistent that the black spectators would have to remain apart from the whites, or they would be compelled to leave the field.

Well, in the end, the police left for a time only to return before the game was over. The whole situation made a big impression on me. Since then, some of my racial experiences have shown me good things while others have shown me bad things. No matter, I always tried to ask myself at such times, "Am I fair to people of all races?"

Despite the above occurrence, I never experienced any confrontations between whites and blacks in my six years at Paine High School and College. The world around the campus was strictly segregated though. When white teachers drove off campus with black students or vice versa, the local police would follow them about until they returned. Integration was only possible within the environs of Paine's campus.

Chapter 4

Easter Finery

ONE OF MY OLDER SISTERS, CARRIE, was teaching school away and always sent us pretty organza and lace dresses for Easter. She was able to do this because she worked at a Presbyterian school in North Carolina supported by wealthy Northern white folks. Sometimes they were new clothes, and other times they were second-hand clothes, but even then they were gorgeous. You see, these clothes included especially expensive dresses and other items of clothing that the white folks' children had outgrown.

Carrie told me how the dresses were folded ever so neatly and packed for shipment to the school in cardboard barrels of varying sizes. Lucky for her, she was always asked by the school officials to help unpack the barrels. As a result, she was allowed to pick out a number of dresses to forward to us in Nuberg. She said the officials and her teaching colleagues knew us by name and all about us because Carrie talked so much about her family.

I felt so excited and happy in my new dress every Easter that I suddenly developed a kidney problem and had to get up from the pew in church and go out three or four times during the preacher's service to the bathroom. Even now, I can still see myself all aglow in a pink organza dress, trimmed in white lace, matching lace socks tucked into black patent leather shoes.

I just knew I looked great in my Easter outfit and that everybody in Norman's Grove CME church was all eyes every time I paraded up and down the aisle. No doubt my mind was more on myself than the good Lord. About the fourth time, I rose to sashay down the aisle, a strong brown arm reached out and sat me back down abruptly. Mama had decided my devilish distractions from the service had gone far enough. Instantly contrite, I knew I would get it after church. My vanity had a price.

Norman Grove CME Church, where Ruth B. Crawford attended the Easter services during her early childhood. The Church was established on September 18, 1880.

Still, as I grew older, I looked forward every year to Easter to wear my new finery. By age 12, I had grown quite tall and skinny and longed for a pair of high heels. I was working hard around the house and farm and figured if I begged hard enough papa would get me high heels—especially as other kids my age were wearing them.

Papa soon gave into my pleading and announced that he would sell a bale of cotton that year to buy clothes to complement Carrie's Easter selections. The bale took up so much room in the wagon, there was no room for me to go to town. Undaunted, I took a piece of string and measured my foot so he'd get the right size.

I kept busy while he was gone, trying to visualize my new shoes endlessly. Finally, he returned, and I tore open the package to find that papa had bought me a pair of black patent leather high heel sandals with cutouts for the toes. Within moments, I had slipped my feet into the shoes. They didn't fit! My toes got balled up and stuck through the holes.

There was no way, though, I was going to give up those high heels. I forced my feet into them and strutted about everywhere despite the pain. My insistence on keeping them demanded a payoff in the form of bunions and six hammer toes. Later, four of my toes would require surgery to correct them. Oh, the folly of vanity.

Sometimes at school, we'd only have one black teacher for the five, six or seven grades. Those times, the teacher had to group the pupils by grades and put some of them in what they called "interest corner," or what are called learning centers today. As the smarter kids learned, they would help the teacher with the other groups of kids.

Boys were always given the task of making the fire every chilly morning in the pot-bellied wood stove. I don't know why the girls couldn't since we had been taught to light them at age six or seven. The parents worked it out among themselves as to who would cut the wood for cold school days.

Much of the wood contributed by parents was what they called "liddiad" in those days—a sort of kindling gathered from the inside of decaying stumps. The stumps were mostly found upon "new ground" land cleared about the low lying areas—often along a creek—and sometimes referred to as the "bottoms." I was always hearing new words like liddiad, and a lot of them didn't make sense to me as a child. No matter, liddiad made good kindling—much like what you buy in small knotted bundles today at the store.

In the small black world then, everybody knew everybody else's business. Even knew a lot of the white folks' business too. Folks would just hear things, bits and pieces sometimes, and just pass it around to be digested like a bite of chicken.

Walking the five miles to school daily provided anyone with open eyes to learn who lived along the route. You got to know how they d be dressed even down to the color of their gowns and pajamas. You'd see who got up early and who lay in bed. Who tended to the farm animals, fed the chickens and who got to do the household chores—the cooking, sweeping and drawing of water.

Other times, when we didn't follow the road to school but opted to wind our way through the woods, other sights would be available to our wondering eyes. Over time, we knew all the names of the vegetation, bushes and trees, especially the pecan and walnut varieties and the sites of the chinky peas. Not a morning passed that we didn't glimpse a wild animal or two. Now and then, we'd even catch sight of a small deer. They hardly paid us any heed as we were as familiar to them as they were to us.

Usually, I walked along just in the company of some of my sisters and our girlfriends. Boys went their own strange way to school, stumbling one way or another into trouble, but other times, a few little boys would be found in our chattering groups. Occasionally, I would let one of them carry my books.

It was a fact, you see, that the Burton girls were something special thereabouts in that period. It's not bragging to note that we were the best dressed girls most of the time and especially at Easter. We were the only family in and around Nuberg who had girls teaching at Flat Rock and in North Carolina. Fact was when Carrie would visit, we always welcomed the chance to ride into town with her just to see how the other black folks reacted to her stylish manner. Some folks thought she talked like a Northerner, but she actually was only speaking good English.

With all the girls in the family, it seemed like some boy or other was forever chasing after my sisters, although I had little interest at that time in boys. Once when one of my sisters, Ida Lois, was teaching me, she had a male teacher, Earl Carter, a young handsome fellow from South Carolina, sweet on her. In a way of sort of courting her, he would walk five miles weekly to visit. He also sought to charm my brothers by bringing things from the city for them like chains and jigsaw puzzles. In return, he'd ask them to walk at least part of the way back with him to his boarding house especially through the wooded portions at night.

One Sunday night, he came out from town with two friends in a new car. Instead of coming to the door, they blew the horn continuously. None of us dared to go to the door to hush them. You see, papa always held these 30-minute praying sessions every Sunday evening, and no one was allowed to leave before they ended.

He was praying most fervently when the horn sounded, and the louder it sounded, the louder he prayed. I whispered to my sister, "Get up and go to the door before Earl leaves."

Papa interrupted his prayer to say, "You better not get up off your knees. Let them city slickers go." Finally, the prayer ended with a three-fold "amen," and my sister dashed to the door to let Earl know she was at home.

Most of the young men who came calling quickly learned to leave at a decent hour on Sunday night to avoid participating in papa's half hour of praying. One night though, Earl was a little slow off the mark. As he sought to duck out, papa waved him to a stop and said, "No, young man, it's too late. You come into this room with us and get down on your knees and pray. You also have a need to pray."

When all had knelt, papa sent up one eloquent opening

prayer. Without letup, he prayed that night—probably for Earl's benefit—for 35 minutes before winding up with his traditional three-fold "amen." No sooner was he finished than Earl was out the door and headed for town on his own. After that he never remained after 10 o'clock on Sunday evening.

Chapter 5

Sweet Times

LIFE ON OUR FARM WASN'T ALL WORK. There was also lots of fun at times. There were so many games to be played—many of them without bats and balls and stuff.

One special game was Hide 'N Seek, and this is the way we played it. You would select a leader to stand at a designated spot and count by fives (five, 10, 15, 20, etc.) until he reached 95, 100. The leader then would call, "All hid." If the answer was a "no," the leader would repeat his count.

After all the children had hidden, the leader would go in search of them. They would watch the leader, and when they thought they could get to home first, they'd break from cover and make the dash to yell, "Home free!" Anytime the leader got to home first, he'd yell, "I caught you!" Then it was that child's turn to count for the next game.

We always thought Hide 'N Seek was great fun because you could play it with boys and girls. Every time the leader began to count, the boys would race to hide with their favorite girl.

Another game we liked very much was the ritual annual searches for birds who had migrated over the wet winters. Their melodious voices seemed to say, "I'm here again,

I'm here again. Come out and welcome me."

Then there was our old horse named Dan. He was so gentle and handsome. Every day, several of us would clamber onto his back and ride him three miles to check the mailbox. He'd just plod along and give us the most gentle ride possible. On Sunday, old Dan would be hitched to our antique buggy, which we kept clean and shiny, and we'd ride off to church with papa or one of the older boys handling the worn reins. I'm sure Dan was proud of his folks because we were dressed up in our best hats and ruffled bows.

Year after year as I grew up, the church services hardly ever changed. Neither did the way the preacher dressed in his black suit with bell bottom trousers and white shirts, lovingly laundered, starched and ironed by church members. Inevitably, he'd preach about what the sisters and brothers had been up to (usually based on gossip) and go on to chastise and admonish them about God's punishment and the horror of hell's fire and those who possibly might get to meet their mamas in heaven. That man would preach until Aunt Lonie began to shout about the coming of the jubilee.

I liked the singing best of all during the service. My own papa was the director of the choir. There was no organ or piano—nothing in the way of a musical instrument—so papa had to heist the hymn beforehand by drilling, "Do, re, mi, fa, so, la, ti, do," to get the right pitch to the delight of us kids. Once warmed up though, that choir could really sing. One of the stars was a young lady named Annabelle, who could sing alto, bass and soprano.

The choir often sang in rounds and individual parts—each member having a chance to sing solo, sort of as a star. Mostly though, Annabelle sang alto solo, then the full choir would sing the chorus, followed by Annabelle again as the bass soloist. Her voice was so lovely when she sang bass that we'd all break out in applause.

When church was over, we'd file out behind mama and papa and say a few words of thanks to the preacher. The boys would then dash around with their pals while we girls chatted with our friends. When papa signaled, we'd all climb into the buggy, and old Dan would carry us home.

One of the best fun times was making sweet syrup from sugar cane grown on our farm. The cut cane would be taken to our so-called syrup mill where stalks would be placed on a round cob and pressed in place by another round stone. Then old Dan, who was hitched to a long wooden arm extending from the mill, would go round and round grinding the juice out of the cane. Dan's plodding made a perfect circular road in the field. Packed down by his hooves, the track of red clay was surrounded by high grass and exotic colorful weeds and took on the appearance of a lovely wild garden.

Some days, we ground cane with only a few rest periods for old Dan from six o'clock in the morning until five o'clock in the evening. The constant grinding squeezed the pumming, which resembled straw, out of the cane stalks, and it poured out of the back of the mill to mount into a big soft pile. After the mill shut down for the day, we played an assortment of games in the towering pumming, including Hide 'N Seek, London Bridges and Ring 'Round the Roses.

Papa kept a watchful eye on the juice as it filled the cane barrel and at proper moments would pour the contents into a large copper trough designed to cook the juice into syrup. A huge fire was kept going under the trough to cook the juice for seven or eight hours. Papa would have several men help him with the cooking, and they used big copper spoons to skim off the hot juice and pour it into a series of large cans. The initial skimmings were green colored and were set aside for the hogs. When the syrup in the trough began to turn brown, it was skimmed off again for use in making candy.

Happily for us, the peanuts on our farm were ready to

be harvested at the same time as we made the syrup. During the day, the women folk would go into the fields and pull up the peanut plants whose roots were loaded often as not with peanuts. As they brought in the big burlap bags bulging with plants, all of us would join in to pick the peanuts off them.

Fact, I can still hear my mama calling out, "Children, if you want good candy tonight, you'd better stop playing and come help pick peanuts."

The peanuts then were cooked in the shells or hulls as they were called. While they were cooking, you kept tasting them to see if they were ready. When set, you took them out of the pan and shelled them.

Since the skimmings were being recooked as candy later in the evening, we would drop in peanuts galore and cook the candy for a while longer. Once it was almost done, we'd take a handful of the candy and pull it into lengthy taffylike strips that took on a beautiful golden hue. When completed, we patted it out in pans to completely cool and harden.

By the time everything was ready, never was there such tasting and sampling. Mama bragged about papa's syrup and he bragged about her candy. In my mind, they both were delicious. Indeed, every year papa's "Brother Burton Syrup" won first place at the county fair. It was a title he retained as long as he made syrup. As for our candy, it was never in competition because we always ate it before fair time.

Every year at that time, our neighbors would catch the aroma of the syrup and come over to visit and obtain their share of the sweet candy. They'd come early and sit around watching the hot coals and flames heat the big trough in which the syrup and candy were cooking. It was such a fun time every year—especially for us kids because we got to stay up late and mix and mingle with the grown folks.

Later, after we moved to August, when my father died, we requested a brief ceremony at our old country church because mama was suffering from a heart condition and a longer one would be a strain on her. By then, too, we had been living in Augusta for several years, and our church-going habits had changed. In any case, the minister agreed to our request although the choir was unhappy that it wasn't permitted more time to show its respect and fondness for Brother Burton as the members called him.

A few days after the service, we got an invitation from the minister and choir members to participate in another ceremony for papa—one planned for Brother Burton by the choir. This second informal service was scheduled from ten a.m. until four p.m. on Sunday. We were unable to attend, but my sister-in-law, Pearlie, and other relatives and friends back home went to the service.

Pearlie provided all the details afterward. She said the choir sang everyone of papa's favorite hymns and that Annabelle sang soprano, alto and bass. Later, Annabelle talked movingly about papa and how she believed he was smiling in heaven and then broke into tears. Pearlie said she'd never heard such screaming and crying and carrying on in that church for anyone like for papa. Afterward, there was a big picnic outdoors.

Chapter 6

High School Days

WHEN I WAS READY TO ENTER HIGH SCHOOL, old Gene Talmadge had wound up two terms as commissioner of agriculture and was ready to pursue his first term as governor of Georgia. By that time, Talmadge had figured out the formula for his success—nail down the rural vote and put together a state organization loaded with your relatives and friends. With the Great Depression leading the nation into an economic despair for a decade or more, he found Wall Street and financial institutions easy to target as the enemies of the farmer.

At that time, I remember mama and papa talking worriedly about the bad times and how many people were being forced off their land by the banks. All around them, they could see the impact on the farmers, small businessmen, and mill workers of the loss of jobs, low wages, and the migration of native Georgians to the North. Many farms had also been abandoned and cotton fields left barren because of the infestation of the boll weevil insect throughout the twenties and into the thirties.

I remember how we fought the boll weevils for years to

save our cotton. That's when I really started to learn how hard it is to live. Those insects were incredible the way they ate up the crop. You'd go to pick off the cotton balls, and they'd be half eaten or gone completely.

Those were the years when you had to live on whatever you had managed to save from the year before. No matter, I never remember going hungry. You see, living on a farm, we could always grow foods for ourselves and at least put something in our stomachs even if it was turnip greens and peas. No way the folks in the city could plant a garden big enough to feed themselves. Those were the hardest of times for everybody, and they lasted for years.

No, it was no picnic then. Georgia was no longer the Empire State of the South. The state was dry and fell easy victim to the moonshiners making white lightning in their stills in the hills. Fact was, they were the only people with money during the Depression. The biggest one in Hart County was my brother, Lafayette or Fate, as we called him. Many times, I heard Fate tell how other moonshiners would put old car batteries in their stills to make the mash quicker.

I warned folks not to buy their liquor from other moonshiners because you never knew what they put in it. Fate made only the best white lightning. If anyone was arrested for drunken driving, all he had to do was tell Sheriff Harper that he had bought his booze from Fate Burton, and he'd be let go. The reason for this was that Fate and the white sheriff were partners in the still. The sheriff even donated any liquor he confiscated from other stills to Fate's operation. They always split the profits 50-50.

This went on for years with both of them making lots of money until the federal men were sent into the area to stop the flow of illegal liquor. They began to search all of the farms thereabouts and finally came to Fate s place. Going through the motions, Sheriff Harper participated in these searches, always bringing along his young son.

Sheriff Harper, of course, knew exactly where Fate hid his liquor under the hay-covered barn floor but was careful to lead the federal men around the hiding spot. The searchers were about to leave the barn when little Johnnie Harper began jumping up and down on the floor and cried out, "Daddy, look in here. I think there's something under the boards."

Well, the federal men poked about and found the trap door leading down into Fate's stash of liquor, and shortly my brother was on the way to jail. Fate was found guilty and fined. The sheriff paid his fine and told him not to start up the still because he no longer could protect him from the federal men.

I remember when Fate died. He had one of the biggest funerals ever held thereabouts and Sheriff Harper led the procession of mourners into the church. He sat with the family and openly wept during the service and even got up and delivered a very moving eulogy, saying Fate was "like an old house whose exterior needed painting but whose interior held a heart of gold." Kind of a mixed up metaphor, but his intentions were well meant.

Our roads were the worst in the South, and the state resorted to the infamous road gangs to keep them somewhat passable. Sadly, just as I was entering high school, we heard that our schools, black and white, were regarded as the worst in the then 48 states.

I thought of myself as a country girl, and it was a big step for me to get a chance to go to a city school. It was the Hart County Training School located in the county seat of Hartwell. Going there meant I had to stay at a boarding house near the school and only go home on weekends.

To prepare myself, I had worked diligently to pass all my subjects in the lower grades. Since my sisters had gone to college, it was just expected that I would follow in their footsteps. I thought it was a great idea to go to Hart County Training and then college because it meant I wouldn't have to pick cotton after school every day. Another thing was my parents had bought me new clothes for high school, and I couldn't wait to wear them. They weren't as pretty though as the ones my sister Carrie had sent us from the Presbyterian school.

Anyway, I went off to Hartwell and put up at the boarding house almost next to the school. Papa noticed a nearby jukebox joint and cautioned me to keep my windows closed so as not to hear the music. I guess he thought it would shock me after so many years of listening to the beautiful music from his church choir.

Professor Fant was the black principal of the school. He was a professor more by vocation than by education since he had only finished high school. Still, you learned quickly that everybody looked up to Professor Fant and his wife, Miss Fanny—never Mrs. Fant or Miss Fant. She was this big, fat, lazy woman who had the students do everything for her in both the school and the dormitory.

Miss Fanny was not educated enough to teach any class, but she was smart enough to get the professor s prized students to dress her every morning. Even when the Fants were going out late in the day or evening, a student would come around to perform this chore. Most of the time, though, Miss Fanny sat in a big stuffed chair and admired herself in a large lovely mirror as well as in an oversized revolving hand mirror.

When sent to help her, you had to get her makeup and fan her while she proceeded to beautify herself. She'd put on three coats of paints and another three layers of powder to give herself a grotesque clownish appearance. Then you had to hold the mirror to the back of her head so she could powder her neck and make sure everything was proper back there.

If that wasn't enough, the student had to tell her all the while how beautiful she was. You had to stay there, too, while she called Professor Fant, and he came into the boudoir to tell her how beautiful she was. I must say she did have a very pretty face, but if she'd only have done something about all those blobs of fat. There was an understanding that she and her husband would never mention her size.

Two of my teachers at Hart County Training were recent graduates of Paine College in Augusta down in Richmond County. One was Clara Williams (later Clara West) and the other George Bryant. Miss Williams wasn't much older than some of her students, but I considered her a good teacher—sort of our mentor. I must say she was proud and prim and always dressed properly—as Professor Fant would point our constantly. As a result, she enjoyed special attention from the faculty and the students.

Miss Williams specialty was home economics, and I had a hate-love relationship with the course. I m sure you can tell by now that I love stylish clothes, but there was a time at Hart County Training when I was ready to tear up my wardrobe. It came about because you had to make a silk pongee shirt before completing the second year of home economics. I just couldn't get the hang of how to sew on the collar. Ten times, at least, I must've ripped the collar off to sew it back on again. Finally, when I had just about given up hope, Miss Williams accepted my shirt for a passing mark.

Miss Williams designed and made most of her clothes, and we all sought to learn how she did it. A feature of her course was to pick a student to model her own clothing and then critique the outfit for us.

It was a truly glorious day when she picked me to have my clothes analyzed. I can remember now that I was wearing a cotton flowered print dress that had been especially made for me by one of my sisters-in-law. You see, going to high school was special among country folks, and the family members wanted to be part of helping you get there. Pearlie, my sister-in-law, loved to sew for just anybody and would devote every minute possible after the lengthy revival meetings in August to making clothes for those going to high school.

She had really spent a lot of time on this special dress I was modeling for Miss Williams. It was an A-line type which really fitted my tall slim form in a nice way. The collar was trimmed in a two-color braid of yellow and brown to complement the printed flowers. It was a special dress for me, and I felt special standing up before the whole class.

I just smiled when Miss Williams called me Janie Ruth and asked me to walk up and down in front of the class. She was always emphasizing how important posture was in making a good appearance and complimented me on my tall figure and ladylike walk. She said that tall people looked much better if they stood tall and held their shoulders erect and head up.

Her comments sure raised my self-esteem because I had always enjoyed being both tall and black. All my life I have stood tall and proud no matter what the situation.

All these years later, I keep fighting to stand tall although I find it harder and harder as I get older. When I let my shoulders droop, I try to think of Clara West and Dr. Clark, who were kind and helpful to me when I was hospitalized for a spell. Dr. Clark would scold me when I didn't want to make the effort to stand and chide me, "All right, heads up and shoulders back. Now get up and walk down the hall." It's truly a task to stand tall now, but I can still talk myself into doing it.

Dear Miss Williams also taught social studies which consisted mostly of her telling us how to associate and react with others—mostly members of the opposite sex. Instead of teaching sex education, she told us female students that it was not a smart idea to hang out with boys. She repeatedly said that men only wanted to marry virgins for wives. She insisted that it was a disgrace and immoral to have sex before marriage.

Her ideas on the subject pretty much were those we heard in church all the time. We all were aware that if a young girl got pregnant, she was put out of the church and dropped from the church rolls. After the baby was born, the girl could return to the church, ask for forgiveness and be re-enrolled.

Despite this knowledge, we all fantasized among ourselves if Miss Williams would eventually have sex with Mr. Bryant, who was young and energetic and taught algebra. I m not sure he knew algebra very well because he would return to his desk often to check his notes. I later found out that he worked the problems out in advance or had someone work them out for him.

He seemed to like all his students very much but insisted that all the girls act lady-like. In my case, he said I was the fast one and my sister, Costella, was the lady. Later, when he got married, he named his first girl after Costella.

One of our main sources of entertainment was to sneak around and peek on Miss Williams and Mr. Bryant when they were together. As soon as one of them left the class, we d rush to see whether the other one was slipping out the back door to keep a rendezvous. Knowing what the teachers were up to was a great opportunity for big talk among ourselves—especially when we didn't see any reason for either Miss Williams or Mr. Bryant to be out of the classroom.

All the time we planned and plotted about what we would do when we grew up and could go out with boys. I guess in a way that our behavior at the time was an early lesson in sociology.

Despite our eternal spying and vigilance, we never saw anything to really talk about. In truth, we only heard doors open and closing discreetly. Those teachers never went out together, and they never returned together.

Professor Fant was our English teacher, but he never taught us anything about grammar, sentence structure or parts of speech. All he did the whole year was to discuss the poem "Thanatopsis" from just about every angle you could imagine. By the time I left at the end of the year, I hardly knew any English grammar or how to spell but had taken my first step to Paine College by making a silk shirt and learning all about Thanatopsis.

I remember Hart County Training School for that one year because it was there that I had my first real boyfriend. His name was A. O. Mance, and he was so handsome and kind. Actually, we never dated since it wasn't permitted, but we would watch and wave to each other in the corridors and halls. At lunch time though, we could sit and talk and grin and plan about the future.

I was to go off to Paine College, where I could finish my last two years of high school before starting college classes, and he was going to Washington, D.C., to look for a job. We would correspond faithfully for several years, but once I started my college courses, we lost interest and the letters stopped coming as we went our separate ways. Still, I shall always remember the image of this tall, neat and sophisticated black man.

We both knew what life would be like for us if we remained in Hartwell. To have any status at all, we would either have to work for the white folks or try to get into the black education field. Then, though, we wanted more from life and chose to follow our dreams—but along separate paths.

Chapter 7

Off to Augusta

WE WENT DOWN TO AUGUSTA to live as a family because one of my sisters who was a teacher bought a house there and gave it to my parents. It was in August, 1933, when I was to leave for Paine College to finish my last two years of high school. Instead of going alone to Augusta, I went with mama and the kids who were still at home. Papa had to stay on to finish the harvest and then decided that he would farm for another year before he came to Augusta. About that time he was 65 years of age and getting on. Three years later, he would pass away and be laid to rest with my grandparents in the Norman Grove Church Cemetery in Elbert County.

Mama had a very limited education when she married young. Fact was, she could hardly read. Yet, her greatest life-long desire was to help us all get an education. She was always hassling papa about moving to Augusta so that we could further our education. My father finally agreed to the move when the house became available for us.

The day we were to leave for the big city, we were all up early and quickly busy at many tasks. Several chickens were caught and plucked for lunch which was very much like a picnic except there was far more food. Then we set about packing what seemed like enough food for months. Items included flour, corn meal, dried butter beans, and corn. You see no one in the family had a job in Augusta, but we intended to survive, and the dried foods would keep us going for a while.

The plan was for papa to continue to supply us with foodstuffs like the above but also with peas, syrup, and beans. He eventually came to Augusta, but he never really liked it. He was country-bred and never lost his love for the land. To him, city life meant eating light bread and baloney like the city folks. To keep him happy in those last years, mama baked him fresh biscuits every day.

You should have seen us when it came time to leave for Augusta. We all piled into a big blue Buick papa had bought for next to nothing in a local junk yard.

One of my brothers knew all about cars and tinkered with it to get it into halfway decent condition. He was no artist when it came to painting the car. He had bought a large can of an awful shade of blue paint and just sloshed it all over the Buick. It was a horrible color. Worst yet, his paint job was just streaked to beat the band.

What a sight we made puttering down that highway to Augusta. There was a country boy at the wheel with mama wearing her apron sitting beside him and giving directions. Even in that hot Georgia sun, mama never wore a bonnet. Instead, she always brushed her long straight hair back over her neck and twisted it into a ball. Wide-eyed and fearful, my sisters, Costella and Lois, and I—buried in a mound of bags and boxes—just hung on for dear life while we roared along at about 30 miles an hour.

I should mention here that my mother was also tall and slim with a light bronze complexion. Her appearance was due to family traits going back to her mother, who had an ebony complexion, and her father whose race was never designated by her. We heard, though, that he was fair-complexioned with blue eyes and straight brown hair and that he had been raised in the home of a white man. After this white man died, family tradition had it, he was sent to live with his darker relatives and married my grandmother. Mama was born from this marriage.

Proudly holding fast to the wheel, my brother was surprised how long he could coast in the Buick after turning off the engine and letting it roll along on its own. All along, he had told mama that it would be an inexpensive trip because he knew how to let the car coast. It was a lot easier to do it on the hills and paved highways than the red clay roads around Nuberg where he had gained his driving experience. It was the first major trip for all of us including mama. We left Hart County about eight o'clock in the morning and arrived weary and dusty ten hours later in Augusta. We were slow getting there because of frequent stops to rest and picnic and to put water in the engine and for all the coasting we did. All was forgotten, though, when we saw our new house which had been professionally built and painted a light brown with a beige trim. The interior walls had been plastered and painted a brilliant white. We couldn't believe a house could be so sparkling clean and bright.

Oh, the joy of our first new house! We felt like we had been given a piece of heaven. For once, we each had our own room. The kitchen boasted running water, and the dining room had a working fireplace. The house also contained an indoor bathroom with hot and cold water so we could bathe every day. No longer did we have to draw water from a well and bath in a tin tub. For the first few months, it was a luxury we all indulged.

Unfortunately, there was a mirror affixed to the wall over the mantel above the fireplace which was to prove a nuisance to my sisters and me. All the time we lived in that house, mama always sat in front of the fireplace so she could see us with any boys who came calling.

Many times she pretended to nod off, but she was as wide awake as a panther watching young lambs. No one could enter the front door without her seeing them. Often times, we would try to sneak into a corner to get out of her view, but she would subtly relocate her chair to keep us in sight. There was just no getting away with anything with her.

My mama was very strict with us children—especially the girls. I remember my first date was a boy named John, who came to the house and was unaware that mother could see us with the help of the mirror when he innocently put his hand on my head.

You should've heard my mother scream: "Get your hands off my girl's head! You just let all the boys know, Ruthie, that I ain't raising no "Fan Foots" around here."

I don't know to this day what mama meant by "Fan Foots" since she never explained. I do know, though, that John left in a rush and never returned. When I met him years later after we both had married, he told me that my mama had scared him near half to death. We enjoyed a good laugh when I explained about the mirror, but only then.

Mama had a strict set of rules for almost every activity in the house—especially about picking up after yourself. One time, she finally gave permission for me to go out to a movie with a new beau named Kenner. It would be the first opportunity to be with a date without mama peeking in the mirror to keep an eye on me.

I was so happy as I dressed and picked out my shoes and squirted on perfume just as Kenner arrived. I dashed out to greet him, and together we started down the walk to the bus stop. Just then, mama came charging out of the house.

"Young lady," she cried loud enough to be heard all over the neighborhood, "you just get yourself back to your room and pick up those dresses and shoes and hang them up properly."

I was so embarrassed, I thought I'd die. Well, Kenner waited patiently on the front porch while I followed mama's orders. All the time she continued to scold me in a voice that just seemed to get louder and louder with every passing moment. It was my impression that she was trying to belittle me in front of Kenner in the hope of driving him away—and any other boys that came calling.

Kenner and I finally got away on our date. He was very attentive, but if mama was trying to give him a message, she apparently succeeded. He never came back after that night.

I decided that I would just keep my distance from boys for a while. Mama's attitude toward them, her strictness with her girls, and that mirror over the mantel were enough to discourage any thoughts of dating just then.

Anyway, after we pulled up in front of our beautiful new home and began to unload all the boxes of food and bags of clothes and household items, we realized that the neighbors were staring at us. I don't think those city folks had ever seen a blue car like ours or croker bags stuffed with food to keep us fed during the coming winter.

I guess I can't blame them for staring. We were a strange looking lot: Mama in her apron, a trio of longlegged girls in dusty and wrinkled gingham dresses, and our brother buried under boxes and bags.

We gave them even more to wonder and laugh about when we began to make the house cozy and comfortable. Back in Nuberg, we only strung ruffled organza curtains over the windows. For the new house, these curtains didn't fit the windows perfectly and people could see inside.

The fact that we didn't have any shades didn't help either. Living in the country back home, we never considered shades, but—there in the city—everybody used them to keep nosy people from looking into their houses. After a bit, we got to know our neighbors and saw the need for shades on all our windows.

Once settled in, we went about the task that had

brought us to Augusta—namely getting ourselves enrolled in a good school for black high school students. Without consulting my older sister, Carrie, a teacher who fancied herself the authority on such matters, we enrolled in Haines Institute, which had been founded in the city in 1886 by Lucy Craft Laney. Haines was considered the top college preparatory school in the area—justly noted for providing the city's first school of nursing which later became the Lamar School of Nursing.

I don't think it was more than a week later that Carrie informed us that we were to transfer to her alma mater, Paine College, because Miss Laney had died earlier that year. She felt that Haines standards no longer would be those demanded by Miss Laney. Paine, at the time, had a high school leading to entry into the college.

My brother was a senior, one sister was a freshman, and I was a junior. City school was a rude awakening for us. The students gawked at us like we were from a foreign planet rather than from the country. They gave us weird nicknames and mocked our clothing and accents.

I especially resented their cruel remarks about my clothes because we always wore clothes that were clean and well ironed even if they were somewhat different from what the city kids wore. I got to hiding my school dresses under the mattress because mama believed in washing, starching and ironing them every night—even if she had to dry them before an open fire. They tended to fade and look different from the city kids clothes whose mamas didn't wash and iron them every night.

Even then kids wanted to conform and belong. I consoled myself with the thought that even if we looked a little different, we lived in the newest and prettiest house in the neighborhood. Soon, we made friends around home and at school and looked forward to a time when the teasing would end.

One of the people I got to know was a young and attractive nurse who lived just across the street from us. She never lacked for boyfriends and often tried to introduce me to boys. For a time, mama was a stickler against my dating, but she finally agreed that I could let one by the name of Marion "Wop" Scott call on me. Marion was familiar to me because he was a friend of Arthur Lee Simpkins, who was calling on a girl named Jenny next door, and I'd see him coming and going.

Arthur later became a noted movie star and sang his famous rendition of "Trees" at President Eisenhower's inauguration. Before becoming a star, he worked for the Georgia Railroad Bank in Augusta with George Singfield, who is a friend of mine to this day. In their off time, they would play and sing in the Golden Delegge Band, which later became known as the Augusta Night Hawks.

One night when Arthur was at the club, Earl "Fat" Hines came by because he had heard that Arthur had a great voice. He asked what key Arthur sang in, and Arthur replied it was C above middle C. Later that night after listening to his voice, Earl Hines hired Arthur to tour the country with him and his group. Stardom followed for Arthur.

After a while, mama even gave me permission to go to a dance with Marion. I had mixed emotions because I didn't know how to dance and really had never seen anyone dance. But once we were at the Duke's Dance, I watched the other couples dance for a while and listened to the music. I figured there wasn't that much to it and got out on the floor and started dancing, and I've never stopped. It's one of life's joys.

Meanwhile, we were still enduring a bit of teasing at the high school until one teacher, Mr. Brown, became aware of the situation and set our tormentors straight. Mostly he stressed the fact that as country children we tended to be reared with more character than city kids and had also experienced greater parental supervision growing up. He said it was easy to see that we had been imbued with a higher set of values than city kids.

Mr. Brown also noted that farming had given us a better insight into many life experiences, taught us many practical talents and crafts, and provided a healthy life. He said he doubted that any of the city kids had been provided day after day with the great nutritious foods that we had eaten home grown and cooked on the farm. He got the city kids thinking about the advantages of country life, and soon most of them came around to respect us and leave us alone.

Mr. Brown became a good friend of the family, and oft time, mama would invite him to Sunday evening dinner. What a dinner it would be! Mama would kill the plumpest chicken in the coop and soak blackeyed peas all night to make sure they were tender and tasteful. The rice would be cooked to perfection with every grain standing apart. She'd even open a jar of chitterlings, the favorite soul food of the South. It was mama's intention to show Mr. Brown genuine appreciation for the respect he had shown her family.

Half a century later, the house is still in the family. Actually, I own it and rent it year after year to folks I know well. It's really not a financial asset because commercial firms surround it and make for higher taxes. Even now, though, when I have occasion to go into the house, I look for mama's mirror and think that some day I'll give it to one of the family. Whoever gets it, though, is going to have to put it over a mantel. Meanwhile, I keep the old house for nostalgic reasons and will ride by it very slowly anytime my sisters, Costella and Lois, come to visit in Augusta. It's stuffed full of wonderful memories.

As I write about chitterlings, I'm reminded of my sister Sarah, who lived in Baltimore. She was the only sister who married young and did not attend college. Her husband's name was Otis, and he worked at a shipyard and got a good week's pay.

Sarah came home every August dressed in her loveliest finery. She always brought a request from Otis that she return with a jar full of chitterlings. This one time she sneaked a lengthy chitterling out of the jar and replaced the cap. To make the jar look full so Otis wouldn't know she had been into it, Sarah shook it up.

Sarah's face was twitching and her mouth was watering with anticipation as she dangled the chitterling before her lips. With a big smile wreathing her features, she bit into the chitterling.

"Ugh! Oh, my God!," she cried. "What an awful taste!" she howled as she sputtered and spat. Unfortunately, and much to our surprise, the chitterling was lined with hog droppings.

We advised her to throw the whole jar of chitterlings away, but she said she couldn't admit to Otis that she had sought to sample his precious chitterlings. I don't remember how the rest of the chitterlings turned out. I do know that every time I visited Sarah thereafter, and she began to criticize me, I only had to inquire whether Otis would remember that particular jar of chitterlings to quiet her.

Chapter 8

Racial Matters

I GRADUATED FROM PAINE HIGH SCHOOL IN 1935 without honors. Frankly, those two years at Paine had been very difficult for me. My studies at Hart County Training and the country schools before that had not provided me with the knowledge and skills to do college preparatory work. I was happy just to graduate from high school and be accepted at Paine College.

Paine had been founded in 1882 by CME Bishop Lucius H. Holsey, a former slave, and named for Bishop Robert Paine. Churchmen of both races had joined forces to sponsor and support the school for blacks—a truly revolutionary proposal for that time—although all qualified students were and are welcomed. First located on Broad Street, the college moved its plant in 1886 to the Woodlawn section of Augusta, its current location. From its beginnings, the student body was black, but the faculty was black and white. Its main mission was to train teachers and ministers. Today, it offers a broad liberal arts curriculum under Christian influences.

One of the key things we all had to do summers between school years was to get a job and save as much money as we could for college. Remember, we had absolutely no money to speak of when we left Nuberg and went down to Augusta. I got myself several babysitting jobs to begin saving money for tuition and books.

One of my very first customers was the white family of Dr. Carver, whom mama got to know being one of his patients. When he learned about mama s serious desire to educate us, he said he would give her all the extra help possible. After that, I always babysat for their little son, Billy, on nights they went out.

I sensed right away that Mrs. Carver was not too happy about the doctor always driving me home; but he had a couple of reasons for doing that. One, he had promised my mother to see me safely home. Two, he had no intention of sending me home with friends of his who might be tipsy after a party.

Dr. Carver was a truly kind man. Often times, he would give me extra money when he knew tuition or books were due. Mrs. Carver asked me once whether he was giving me extra money, and I just looked at her without answering.

Dr. Carver told me, "Anytime I give you a tip, it doesn't matter to me whether you tell my wife or not." He implied that Mrs. Carver didn't understand the value of having an intelligent babysitter who could read to Billy. For myself, I learned very early it was best not to comment in any way on the talk between a man and his wife. Frankly, I felt like they were testing me to see whether I would talk out of turn.

I remember one time they were going out the door and Dr. Carver handed me a note that read: "Mrs. Fairlee is very old, frail and ill. If she calls here, please tell her to call me at the number below, and I will go to her right away. Do not give the number to anyone else."

Sure enough, later in the evening, Mrs. Fairlee's daughter called and asked for the doctor. I gave her the number, and she called him at this party he and Mrs. Carver were attending. Well, they left the party immediately and came back to the house where he could collect his medicine bag.

Mrs. Carver was obviously upset about leaving the party early and demanded to know in a high pitched voice, "How did they know where you were?"

The doctor remained calm and simply said, "I've taken an oath, and I must go to her."

Fortunately for me, he decided that he would drop me off at home on his way to see Mrs. Fairlee. There was no way I wanted to stay in that house and listen to Mrs. Carver going on like a raging inferno.

Another white family I worked for over a summer was the Abbotts, and the members consisted of a mother and father, a four-year-old son, and a grandfather. Their previous day help was a toothless black woman who had taught the child to talk just like her. His favorite expression was "nanny, yar, dar, uh," whatever that meant.

I told little Bobby that my name was Ruth, and he would have to call me by that name, or I would not do anything for him. To test my resolve, he would only utter funny noises and point to what he wanted. In response, I would close my eyes and insist that he tell me in a normal voice what he wanted.

Supposedly, Bobby only knew a few words like, "yelp," "naw," and "Missy." I was determined though, and before the summer was over, Bobby was speaking normally for his age, and we were having a lot of fun playing together.

It was really impressive how much I was able to teach him in the three months we were together. The joy I felt at witnessing his improvement stirred my desire to become a teacher. The experience provided me with a wonderful opportunity to see whether I would like teaching.

I decided that while it could be tiresome, it also was a lot of fun and very rewarding. Bobby, in effect, was my guinea pig to determine whether or not I would become a teacher, but his mother had no awareness of this. I often even taught him two and three syllable words.

It came as a shock then one Sunday as I was serving dinner for the family when Bobby asked his father in perfect English, "Is Ruth a nigger?"

There were a few tense moments without any adult saying a word. We just looked at each other. I pulled off my apron and left the house. Mrs. Abbott came rushing after me, all in a frenzy.

"Please don't go, Ruth," she pleaded. "I can't work without you. Please stay. Bobby's only a child and doesn't know of what he speaks."

I turned to let her have her say. I think this was the first time we had a serious discussion and the opportunity to come to understand each other, somewhat. She praised my work and noted that they never had anyone like me before to work in the house. They were truly fortunate, she said, because I knew how to write checks and balance the check book, shop for groceries and sundries, and plan and cook the meals.

I was very pleased to hear the nice things Mrs. Abbott had to say, but I still never forgot the insult. When I told her shortly that it was time to return to college, she offered to double my salary to nine dollars weekly if I would stay. But I was determined to finish college, and no mint in Washington could print enough money to get me to be a maid instead of a teacher.

Upon realizing that I was not to be deterred from my goal, she begged me if I would teach her how to cook fried chicken before I left. Oh boy, now was my chance to get even. Come Sunday she joined me in the kitchen to watch how I washed the chicken, sprinkled on a little salt and flour, and added a tablespoon of oil to the pan before placing it on the stove to fry slowly. But as soon as Mrs. Abbott left the kitchen, I pulled out the pan, added three cups of oil to the pan, turned the stove on high and fried that chicken to a crisp brown.

Good southern fried chicken has to be cooked in deep fat and cooked rapidly, otherwise it will be soft instead of crispy. Being from the country I knew how to cook fried chicken correctly. In fact, I could cook almost any kind of country food you could name.

Some weeks later, I bumped into Mrs. Abbott when coming from school, and she informed me that she still couldn't get the hang of how to cook fried chicken. I just smiled innocently and told her to stick to my directions faithfully and keep on trying. I think what I really meant was that she should hire a smart cook who could do it for her. I never did hear whether she finally mastered the art of frying chicken.

During this time, I had mixed emotions about white people since I came from a rural area and was the daughter of a sharecropper. My mama had a very dear white friend, Mrs. Moore, who used to come to our house and sit on the porch or in the living room and always take the best chair. I totally resented her doing this and told my mama, "you can't go to her home and do the same thing."

Well, I was proved wrong years later when mama took sick and died while at my sister's home in Anderson, South Carolina. Anyway, her white friend, unaware of the transfer, had brought her some jelly and homemade candy and left them at the back door with a note that read: "Dear Lizzie, I'm worried about you. Please call."

I decided that the right thing to do was to go to Mrs. Moore's house and tell her about mother's death. I dreaded this experience but went anyway accompanied by my five-year-old son, George. She greeted me warmly at the front door, invited me inside, and insisted I sit in her living room that was filled with elegant antique furniture.

I took a deep breath and told her about mama's passing. We just sat there and cried. Later, she served my son and me some of her homemade cake. All the time, I was keeping an eye on little George and cautioning him about getting into anything. Don't do this. Don't do that.

But this lovely lady suggested, "Let the child play. He

surely can't hurt this furniture." She was so sympathetic, I couldn't believe that I once had resented her sitting in mama's best chairs.

When I thought of Dr. Carvers kindness and the hospitality of Mrs. Moore, I came early to respect people for their true worth and not to decide whether they were good or bad, depending on their race. There's good and bad in black and white, and you must never judge a person by his membership in a group or race. You just can't let your emotions twist your objectivity.

This summer, I went to Washington D. C. and we had tickets to go to see "Miss Saigon". This was a great affair for me. (I am still the country girl at heart.) I got all dressed up in my pure linen and lace dress and joined the crowd off to the Kennedy Center. We had excellent seats because my niece works there. After the first half, she carried us to this most beautiful reception room to have tea and coffee, and other sweets. Here, I walked around sipping tea, knowing that I am somebody. I am educated, dressed to the nines and concerned about being accepted. I spoke to a few people of other races. Other members of the group came in and suddenly all of the white people quietly moved out. Oh! Here it is again in the Nation's Capital—Negroes are not good enough; My, My! My mind was at work; segregation at work. Then finally, my niece said, "This is a long intermission." The lounge host answered, "No, the bell sounded a few minutes ago when most people left." Here I go again! Wrong, drawing the wrong conclusion. Everyone was there to see "Miss Saigon" and not concerned about me and others. I was ashamed of my thoughts. Again, we must work together and not be overly sensitive. You must have had similar experiences. After visiting awhile with me in "Teach As If The Woods Are On Fire", I hope you will be open-minded.

You see, I had witnessed vicious whites ready and eager to lynch my brother for something he didn't do. In contrast,

I had met concerned whites who were anxious for me to get every bit of schooling possible. Unfortunately, I guess there'll always be mixed emotions on both sides about race, but I pray all Americans remember that it takes both the black keys and the white keys on a piano to play "America the Beautiful."

Right down until today, I have friends of every race, color, and creed. We respect each other for what we are. Now that I am constantly striving to keep my Shiloh Comprehensive Community Center open, two of my greatest supporters are two fine businessmen, Mr. Boykin and Mr. Tyson, one white and one black.

The basis of all the tales and anecdotes included in my story is to show how one can use wise judgment and cleverness to solve problems. They help eliminate hate and strife.

Chapter 9

Paine College Days

PRESIDENT FRANKLIN D. ROOSEVELT was finishing up his first term as president, and old Gene Talmadge was raising hell in the governor's office in Atlanta when I entered my freshman year at Paine College in 1935. The Depression was felt everywhere—especially by farmers and the workingman. The wealthy were more powerful than ever, the poor more impotent. Decadence was abundant. Pessimism was everywhere.

On entering Paine, we were told that we would remain enrolled only as long as we made passing grades. Once we failed, we would be dismissed and be sent out to work to help others who might succeed in college and pay the family's bills—especially the monthly mortgage. Times were too hard to put up with those not willing to study and work.

One of my jobs was to iron shirts each week for a retired army colonel who paid me something extra so I could buy special rolls at a price of 10 cents a dozen. They were made by a colored man during the thirties who sold his rolls to stores and schools. After a while, his rolls became famous, and they became known as "the colored man's rolls." Unfortunately, he never registered his recipe and couldn't compete when the bread factories began turning out rolls by the thousands. All too soon, he went out of business, and we never heard whether he got a job making rolls with one of the companies or what became of him.

Only Costella and I went to Paine College. My sister, Lois, graduated from Mary Potter High School in North Carolina, where Carrie taught. Carrie then sent her to Fayetteville State College in North Carolina. My brother, who had graduated from Paine High School, decided that since three of his sisters would be in college simultaneously, he would go to Detroit and try to find work.

I was given a work-study job, and my supervisor was a teacher named Fred Lynn. I did various tasks for him in the sociology department and also around the house trailer he occupied with his wife, Penny. One uninhibited character, Mr. Lynn, taught sociology based more on his personal life experiences than from any textbook. A lot of observations were related to experiences he had gained traveling around the world as a self-professed hobo.

Since Mrs. Lynn did not know how to cook—can you believe it?—I was brought in to prepare the meal and set the table. My meals, I have to admit, sometimes were queer, but the grownup guests seemed to enjoy them.

I remember one time Dean Steely and his five-year-old son, Willy, came to dinner. As was the custom, Mrs. Lynn asked me to serve green turtle soup followed by an entree of stewed frog legs. Just as I was ladling out the soup, young Willy asked his father, "Dad, do I have to eat this nasty green stuff again?"

Dean Steely and his wife were very particular about protocol and good manners, insisting that young Wiley always be a gentleman. That meant that he had to sit up at the table, place his napkin in his lap, use his utensils correctly, and eat everything on his plate. I understood why he didn't want to eat the green turtle soup again and replaced his serving with a small dish of fruit.

Paine College Days

Dean Steely was another unforgettable character. Just about every Paine alumni from those days I'm sure will recall his class. He had some type of Rube Goldberg machine that he claimed could measure the color of our skin from the fairest to the darkest. Everyone in his class was regularly measured, and he would then take great pleasure in telling us the average color for the class and who had the lightest and who had the blackest skin.

Dean Steely was also big into the genealogical field and would ask us to try to trace our ancestors. I don't know how he ever thought we were going to do it for there were few written records about blacks going back before the Civil War. No matter, he insisted that most of us could claim ancestors who were Indian and white along with our black heritage. I thought it was a very interesting theory, but I never had the time to pursue it.

At Paine College, I remember the first lesson in integration as told by Dr. William Graham, one of the vice presidents. It seems that one day a fine white man by the name of Mr. Parnell, who represented the Methodist Church, and his four-year-old son came to visit. Sticking to protocol, he formally introduced himself to Dr. Graham and shook his hand. He then said, "This is my son, David," and instructed the child to shake hands.

As the boy moved to do so, he suddenly screeched, "No, Daddy! No! His hand is dirty." He stared wide-eyed at Dr. Graham's black hand.

Mr. Parnell was appalled at his son's reaction and dropped his head in deep embarrassment. But Dr. Graham rose politely to the occasion and extended his hand to the boy.

"Look, David. See my hand. Feel how smooth it is like yours. You see God made me this color, but you and I have the same color of blood."

Reassured, the boy took his hand and smiled up at him, remarking, 'Since that's so, we can be blood brothers."

Another teacher, I remember, a white one in this case,

was Miss Ruth Bartholomew, or "Belly Whop," as we called her. In my sophomore year, she was my English teacher, and I was her work-study student in the library. I looked forward to this assignment because I had maintained a B plus average in Mr. Steely's course when his work-study student and determined that I could achieve an A or B as a work-study student for Miss Bartholomew.

Well, the weeks passed, and it was test time. She examined my papers and gave me an 84 which amounted to a C plus in those days. I hit the ceiling, believing that I had done much better and had been very helpful to her in the library. I stormed into her office and told her just what I thought: She was just like other white folks who hated Negroes. In my anger, I told her that I could only visualize all the white folks who had tried to lynch my brother and who had done unkind things to my family or me. I sat in her office irate, disappointed, and very resentful of Miss Bartholomew. I think mostly because she was white.

Surprisingly, she never said a word or interrupted me in any way while I ran on about her unfairness to me. When I finally ran out of breath and words, she gazed quietly at me and said, "You have spoken, young lady, and now it is my turn to speak. Whether you agree or not, I graded your paper just like everyone else's. You made an 84, and that is a C plus. That's what you earned, and that's what you got."

Without ever raising her voice or becoming emotional, she continued: "Do you think that I gave up other offers to come to Paine College to mistreat you or any student here? It just isn't so. Don't you know that I could have been much better paid at another school, but I chose to come here?"

When I didn't answer, she gazed at me with sad eyes. "Now I have to wonder whether I wouldn't have been treated better and appreciated more at another college. You must understand that the only way I can sincerely help you students is to do what is honest and right when it comes to evaluating your work. If at the end of the next six weeks, you make an 87 on your tests, then I'll give you a B. But you have to earn it."

It was then that I realized it was her strict character and not any prejudice that guided her actions.

During my years at Paine College, I had several memorable boyfriends, and none more so than Penrose Park, who was an outstanding athlete, very handsome, pleasant, and an avid girlchaser. At one time, he was dating me and another Paine co-ed simultaneously unbeknownst to both of us. He was such a weasel he even managed to take both of us to the same prom even though she lived on the campus and I lived at home with mama in the house on Heard Avenue.

He took Kay Love to the prom at eight o'clock and then came to my house at 8:30 to accompany me on the bus to the prom. When we got there, he left me with his friends while he said he had to go to the bathroom. All night long, he danced alternately with me and Kay Love, skipping back and forth from my table to hers.

I didn't think it was too strange because he was a big athlete, and he and his pals were always huddling to recount past glories in various corners of the big dance hall. Then when he excused himself to dance with someone else as an obligation, I accepted that excuse because my dance card was also filled. I just loved to dance and didn't notice that his "obligation" only extended to one other student.

After the prom, I insisted that he take me home, and we rushed to the bus stop only to miss the bus. He wanted to call a cab, but I argued in favor of walking the mile and a half to my house. On the way, the bus came along, and we hopped aboard. Unfortunately for Penrose, the bus was going back to the depot for the night, and no other would be coming along. He wound up walking back to the campus.

Well, the next morning, the news was flying all over the campus that Penrose was in a lot of trouble with Dean Gray, who supervised the conduct of the students who lived on campus. Kay, tired of waiting for him to return from whatever make-believe place he had gone to, walked alone back to her dormitory. The school rules called for the male to sign out the female student and to return to the dormitory and sign her in.

For committing this serious infraction of the rules, Penrose was barred from dating any girl on campus for two weeks. With my competition out of the running temporarily, he became very attentive and spent a lot of time in the next two weeks at my house on Heard Avenue. On campus, though, I saw very little of him, figuring I would rather not be seen in his company by Dean Gray. During that period, he promised that I would be his one and only. Oh, yeh.

No sooner were the two weeks up than I received a message from Kay informing me that Penrose was back dating her from five to eight p.m. before coming out to Heard Avenue on the bus at 8:10. She also made it a point to tell me that he had written her love notes during the probationary period. I challenged her on that assertion and informed Penrose that if it was true, he was out of my life. He denied it all, but Kay let me glance at the notes, which were in his handwriting, although she wouldn't let me read them. I respected her for that because I understood the contents were of a personal nature.

Anyway, I quickly put Penrose on skates figuratively and rolled him right out of my social life. He wrote me notes almost daily, but I heard that he was continuing to see the other girl from five to eight. He was out of my life, and I let him know it in no uncertain terms.

My love was something I could always control like turning a water spigot on and off. You treat me unfairly, and it was turned off tightly. Because of this ability to control my emotions, I knew that I could never be mistreated by any man or be abused by any husband. That type would just be out of my life.

In my senior year I dated another dark handsome student who helped deliver the Augusta *Chronicle*. Virgil Benson was sweet, protective, and a man of his word unlike Penrose Parks. Our friendship lasted until I graduated and through my first year as a teacher. That last year at Paine, my girlfriends and I did nothing but study and talk about our boyfriends.

I had dated another fellow in my middle years at Paine, but he had graduated ahead of me and was teaching in Bainbridge. He was handsome and tall, but I had enough control of myself so I could take him or leave him. He wrote regularly at first, but then his letters came infrequently. I figured he had found a new love and wished him well.

While I was at Paine, my favorite subjects were sociology and English. Those were always my best subjects. I didn't do as well in history and geography and had no talent at all in the sciences. My school years in Nuberg and Hartwell had prepared me poorly for college work. I would never have made it in the sciences, and I knew it, and that's why I worked extra hard to get good marks in my favorite subjects.

The summer I graduated from Paine with a Bachelor of Arts degree was mostly spent writing applications for a teaching job. Now and then though, I'd babysit for Dr. Carver because he had been so kind to me. Mrs. Carver continued to be something else because she thought his money permitted her to get away with just about anything with people.

I remember one day when I was there that a very sick black woman came to the house to see Dr. Carver at the direction of his office. Mrs. Carver directed her outside to wait in the garage until he could see her. No way did she want that black woman in the house any longer than necessary.

Dr. Carver was very upset when he was informed that the patient had been waiting in the garage. He reminded Mrs. Carver again about the oath he had taken to help people. He read her the riot act up and down. I could only murmur to myself, "Thank God for white people who put human suffering above color."

Once Dr. Carver even told me that his wife was endangering his practice. He had to ask her what would people say or do if a sick person died in the family garage.

Another time, he said, she told him he looked very tired and asked him whether he had been delivering babies or performing abortions.

She was terribly angry especially because she knew that I had overheard this conversation. She was always trying to convince me in so many ways that whites were superior to blacks and was upset when he talked in such a direct manner in front of me. Dr. Carver, though, just told things the way they were.

Dr. Carver was also an avid hunter—especially of small birds and rabbits which he killed for their sweet meat. He'd take his game home and clean it on the front porch. If I was about, he'd call for me to come watch him dissect any rabbit he had killed, noting all the various body parts and the digestive tract in medical terms. It was his way of giving me a biology lesson gratis.

Over time, it became obvious that Mrs. Carver did not appreciate this activity on his part. One day, she finally exploded in a rage and came charging out onto the porch to berate him for it. "What the devil are you doing? You're a doctor. Let Ruth clean those birds and rabbits."

Without raising his voice, Dr. Carver explained that he was prepping me for a biology course I would be taking later that school year. This explanation did not please her at all. She ran into the house to fetch a pot and came running out to toss it full force at him.

Fortunately, Dr. Carver ducked, and the pot sailed overhead. I believe that he would've been killed if the pot had ever struck him. You can bet I went home in a hurry. That house was no place to be when Mrs. Carver was up in arms.

Chapter 10

A Teacher at Last

When I graduated from Paine College, I was given a trip to Boston. I stayed with an older sister, Carrie, who had married John Lindsay, a Jamaican. He had many Jamaican friends but only reluctantly introduced me to one by the name of Wilfist Bliss. With Wilfist, my feelings of love surfaced again. I was much younger than Wilfist, less experienced, and, oh, so country, but did I have fun that summer with him!

Sometimes my sister would permit me to go to various games with Wilfist which I heartily enjoyed. However, most times when his white friends came around and engaged in conversation, I would often go quiet or pick up a book and read. One day Wilfist said, "Why don't you keep right on talking and let my friends see how intelligent you are?"

He also noticed that I had a habit of changing my seat if a young white male sat next to me. I finally had a serious talk with him on this subject and told him about the South and how I had been taught never to get friendly with white men. I explained how some white men would have two families at once, one white and the other black, and how the white community and the white wives had to accept this status without commenting publicly about it. Sometimes even the children in such families were aware that they had half brothers and sisters in the black world.

Accompanied by my sister and her husband, we often went to the beach, and now and then they would let us stroll along the sand without their company. Usually though, it would only be for about 45 minutes. Wilfist was a stickler for the time and always insisted that we rejoin them within the time agreed upon. Let me say that in those 45 minutes we managed to have a lot of fun out of their sight.

In time, we gained their trust so they let me go off with him to pick blueberries at a nearby farm. Little did they know that the farm was the summer home of folks he worked for at times. A blueberry farm was a new experience for me as I had never seen one in Georgia. I always thought blueberries grew on small trees rather than big bushes.

Actually, it was not a big thrill for me to go blueberrying because the bushes were filled with sharp thorns and I use to get scratches on my hands. I liked the berries although I usually ate most of them as I picked them. Back at my sister's home, I'd often eat blueberry muffins and pies.

One time, we did pick blueberries until our pails were full, and then Wilfist asked whether I'd like to see the inside of the house. For the first time, I saw how rich folk lived. The house was just full of beautiful furniture. It was funny though as I gazed about because I could only think what a wonderful place it would be for TB patients who were confined to their hospital rooms all the time.

Wilfist and I were always engaged in small talk for hours on end. Still, he continued to watch the time so we would be home as promised before dark. He was so happy that the family trusted me with him that he did everything in his power to be the perfect gentleman.

I remember saying, "Wilfist, don't you wish we could bottle up this cool country air to take to the hot humid city?"

He replied, "No, no, my dear. Don t you know that if the air could be bottled, the rich would buy all of it, and you and I could not breathe."

Always, we reached home all too soon and Wilfist would be on his way. After he left, I'd just sit on the doorsteps and daydream. I had never known such bliss.

I'm not sure how but sometime in August my sister let it slip to mama that I was dating a Jamaican and wanted to get a job in Boston and stay there. Mama hit the ceiling and told my sister, "You send Janie Ruth home. I want her to teach school, not to marry now."

I was heartbroken and told Wilfist. We had never discussed the possibility of marriage, but at that moment he sort of proposed, noting that "I haven't much to offer but my love."

I knew from mama's teachings and experience that love was not enough to keep a marriage going. I went home, a bit crestfallen and missing Wilfist, but once back in my own surroundings, I knew our love was not to be. Very soon, we stopped writing, and I concluded that our relationship lacked the strength to stand the test of time and separation.

Back home I hurried to check the mail each day in hopes of finding a favorable reply to my applications. Finally, I was offered a teaching job at Washington High and Elementary School in a place I'd never heard of—Blakely, Georgia. I looked for it on a map, and it wasn't even shown. No matter, mama insisted that I accept the offer because she had seen me educated to teach.

At the time, I wasn't sure that's what I wanted to do. The army had just opened Fort Gordon, and Augusta was filled with young soldiers, many of them attractive black recruits. I thought it would be a fun idea to apply for one of the many jobs open for civilians at the installation.

Mama was adamant that I would teach. I can hear her still saying "Positively not!" to my desire to stay at home and work at Fort Gordon. Accepting defeat, I began to pack to go to Blakely. No new clothes were included because my last bit of extra cash had gone for a class ring.

I remember that in 1939 stylish women wore short dresses, high-heel shoes, and short hair. The main dances were the Cha-Cha and the Blackbottom.

Even now, I can see myself in my prize favorite suit—long coat, short skirt with a blue and white scarf draped over the shoulders. How I was going to strut my stuff as a new teacher in Blakely. How I had been waiting for the day when I would be my own boss, making my own money, and spending it as I desired. With my trunk and a few boxes packed with my clothes and things, I awaited the day for my departure.

I bid mama and my two sisters still at home a tearful farewell and boarded the bus for the long ride across the breadth of Georgia to the southwestern section of the state below Columbus, where Blakely was situated. Mama had packed me a goodly supply of fried chicken because in those segregated days, blacks couldn't go into the white folks restaurants to eat and just never knew when you might find a place that fed blacks. Fortunately, the bus did make stops where they had toilets for "coloreds." But even those were few and far between and were usually pretty dirty.

Of course, the buses weren't air conditioned, and clouds of red clay dust streamed through the open windows. It was a long, hot, and lonesome ride, and it seemed as if we went through every briar patch, hill and dale in the U.S.A. When we pulled into Blakely, I was the only passenger still on board. By that time, I was a sight to behold.

Did my pride ever take a bruising when I got off that bus and saw the extent of downtown Blakely. It consisted of the bus stop, a drugstore, a grocery store, and one clothing store. Not far distant was this great big house where the new teachers were to room for the school year under the thumb of what they called in those days a Jean s supervisor, a teacher who checked on the personal life and conduct of her younger colleagues. Later, I was to find out that our supervisor was an old biddie, and we were her chicks. For the moment though, as I gazed in dismay at my new home, I wondered what had brought me to such a past.

When I arrived in Blakely, I was assigned with three other new teachers to a big room with two beds in the big house. There was a well for water, and the bathrooms were also outside, and we had to use those big galvanized steel tubs for baths. I shrugged my shoulders, vowed to accept my fate quietly, and unpacked my trunk and boxes to settle in.

Unhappily, it turned out that one of the quartet of new teachers was very lazy. See, she was cute. Her father was a doctor which impressed the school staff, and she became the pet of the Jean's supervisor, Miss Bessie. Her name was Charlene, and she was so lazy that she wouldn't go to the well to draw water for her bath. Instead, she'd wait until we heated our bath water on the pot belly stove and poured it into the big tins, and then she'd hold up her towel to soak in the steam. When it cooled a bit she would use the towel like a giant face cloth to wash herself.

Initially, we all took turns shopping and cooking meals, but when she began to date the school principal, he'd often take her out to eat dinner. Shortly she stopped shopping and cooking. Fine with us. We just told her she couldn't eat with us anymore.

She apparently went off and cried to Miss Bessie, the Jean's supervisor, who called a meeting to straighten us out. But before she could begin haranguing us, we spilled the beans on Charlene—telling about how lazy she was in not doing her fair share of the chores. Miss Bessie didn't like hearing such things about her pet, but we didn't care.

I must say that I have never forgotten Miss Bessie. In my mind, she was filled constantly with evil thoughts about others and was always using her authority to boss us. At the time, Jean's supervisors got it in their heads that it was part of their duty to keep young teachers in line with the demands of the school system. In fact, they were supposed to supervise our teaching skills not to tell us how to deport ourselves all the time.

I've always believed that she quickly felt threatened by the new teachers because we were college graduates like her. Previously, she had always gotten to pick her teachers from high school graduates. I think she truly felt threatened with too many young, intelligent, and pretty ladies about the school. We were not her little girls. It was all so strange to Miss Bessie.

The poor thing never had a boyfriend. She was just too hard on the eyes. Her teeth, sadly, were crooked, and she squinted. She constantly wore a sly grin on her lips as if she were saying, "I've got you in my web." The insides of her hands were black, and she was forever talking with them.

We always listened without comment when she laid down various rules. Fearing we were not paying attention, she would say, "If you want to stay here and work, you'd better listen. I know what the officials here want."

Even then, we would not answer. For the first time, she was supervising teachers who had finished college. It was a new and frightening experience for her. We could've been sympathetic if she showed any sensitivity at all, but she couldn't change her ways.

As the school year progressed, Miss Bessie continued to lecture us as if we were children. We continued to listen and declined to reply. It seemed as if she, along with the education chairman, Mr. King, was determined to rule our every action.

We accepted this style of authority until she told the young men who came calling that they were not welcomed to visit as long as we lived in her house. We could date, of course, but we could not have male company in the house. Well, by then, we all had boyfriends and were not about to put up with this new rule. We reminded her Charlene would have Mr. Ellis by for company whenever "he jolly well pleased."

Her response was that Mr. Ellis' visits were okay because he was, after all, the principal. I said, "Fine, but my boyfriend should be allowed to visit because his father was the vice president of the Board of Education in Blakely." Another teacher pointed out that her boyfriend was a fellow teacher from another school, and he should be shown the same courtesy as the principal.

Again and again, we met with her to discuss the rules she would arbitrarily impose. We'd argue repeatedly but she had never consented to treat us as adults. She saw us only as the high school graduates she used to supervise.

Seeing how her mind worked, we decided to do something no other teachers had ever done at Blakely: Move out of Miss Bessie's. We looked around and determined that there was only one other big house in town that could accommodate us and that was owned by the town's only electrician, Mr. Swett, a black man.

At first, Mr. Swett hesitated to take us in—I suspected because of local politics. But his wife, Miss Rosa, took up our cause, saying, "It's time for more change in this town. I will be glad to have these young teachers live with us."

Once that was settled, Mr. Swett helped us plan our move. He arranged for a driver with a mule and a wagon to haul our stuff away when Miss Bessie wasn't around. Wouldn't you know it? We ran right into her on the way, and she stood in the middle of the narrow dirt road and ordered the driver to turn the wagon around and take us back to her house.

Well, he didn't know which way to turn until the four of us demanded that he go on to the Swetts house. When he flicked the mule's haunches with his whip, the animal darted forward, and Miss Bessie smartly stepped aside. Still, she followed along to see where we were going and didn't leave us until we turned into the lane leading up to the Swetts' place. Actually, there was not much she could do since Mr. Swett was a member of the local black power structure, being the only electrician thereabouts.

Chapter 11

Coming of Age

YOU HAVE TO REMEMBER THAT IN THOSE DAYS there was a black world and a white world—much like there still is today—and members of these worlds seldom crossed the borders of the other even if they shared the teaching profession. If you knew your world and remained mostly within it, there was little to be resentful about since you dealt mainly with other black folk.

The chairman of the Board of Education was black, the trustees were black, and all the teachers and principals were black in the schools in our world. Only the superintendent of schools was white, and you had little chance to resent him because you seldom saw him. I should mention, too, that all the churches I attended were black and so were all the ministers.

The chairman of the Board of Education was Mr. King, and he was anxious for black folks to know that he was a big man. He always drove to school on opening day in a big white Cadillac to point out his grandchildren to the teachers. Mr. King didn't like me from the "git go" because I informed him in no uncertain terms that his granddaughter, who had been assigned to my class, would be treated the same as the rest of the students.

It was at that point that he decided to begin my "schooling" by instantly reminding me that he ran the town where blacks were concerned. He said no teacher fresh out of college and from far away was going to get uppity with him. He was so put out that he told Miss Bessie to tell me that I was wearing my dresses too short, even though that was the style in the fall of 1939. I told her she could tell him that I'd wear my dresses as I pleased.

Soon after that, I bumped into Mr. King in the local black cemetery, and he growled, "Young lady, your dress is too short." I snapped right back, "Mr. King, my mama bought me this dress, and she saw me in it before I left home and had no fault with it. I'm going to wear the clothes I brought here. Furthermore, if I ever let you buy me a dress, then I'll let you decide on the length."

Mr. King was totally shocked because no one had ever dared talk to him like that before. I even went on to tell him, "I hope my dresses don't continue to upset you because I am in full command of my body and how I will clothe it and don t even think about being tempted by it."

I could see that he was irate, but he just turned about and walked away. I'm sure he wanted to fire me, but the vice president of the school trustees was very fond of me, and I'm sure he defended me. You see, I was dating his son and was often in his home.

It occurred to me very quickly, though, that Mr. King was a powerful man in Blakely, but I was determined not to be intimidated by him. Still, I was nobody's fool and began putting aside some savings from my very first paycheck. I learned early that you needed money to be independent and out from under the thumb of the bosses. Without money, you're at the mercy of other folks.

I would get an example later of just how powerful Mr. King was in that town and also how he had a kind side that he kept hidden most of the time. It happened that one of my roommates got a call in the middle of the night that she should come right home because her mother was dying. Well, none of us had any big money so I suggested that Darlene call Mr. King and see what he could do for her. Never mind it was so late. Mr. King wasted no time in rousing the local banker and going to the bank where they met Darlene, opened the bank to get her some money, and sent her home on the first bus.

When I reported to the school, I was assigned to a first grade class although I had been expecting to teach at the high school level. My sort of mentor was Marian Perkins, a fine young lady from New Orleans, who had graduated from Xavier University. She was well-versed in teaching first and second grade, and realizing I was a novice at teaching at that level, she helped me with my teaching method at night on her own time.

There were so many things I hadn't learned about teaching at Paine and welcomed her assistance. I had no awareness, for example, of how flash cards were used to instruct lower grade school children. Miss Marian was just great, and we got along real well and became good friends.

The black people about Blakely were eager to learn. You could almost say they had a thirst to acquire knowledge. We were the first college-trained teachers except for the Jean's supervisors to come to Blakely and teach their children.

In truth, Blakely was a queer little town. We no sooner had arrived than we were told that black people were not to be seen about on election day. We were also informed—not so subtly—that we had to turn off our lights on election night. Can you believe it?

The fact was that the black people thereabouts were very scared and took these matters seriously. In fact, they were somewhat intimidated and kept in line because of lynchings that had occurred before our arrival.

Well, we new young teachers—four females and two males—weren't going to put up with those traditions. We were young enough and brave enough—probably foolish enough, too—to believe that no one was about to hang us if we went about on election day and burned our lights. Fact is, on election day, we purposely walked about downtown and left the lights burning in our rooms at the Swetts' big house. Nothing happened.

When we walked to school the next morning, black people came out to give us a big smile and told us how much they appreciated our action. Some even seemed to worship us as though we were the most courageous people in the world. Others implied they were ready to shake off their chains of bondage, and maybe we were the leaders they were looking for.

Far as the lights went, we figured nobody would be foolish enough to shoot them out. After all, Mr. Swett was the only electrician in town and the only one available to fix the town lights or any other lights. It wouldn't make much sense to shoot out his lights. As for us, he never said a word one way or the other about burning the lights or turning them off. We noticed, though, that thereafter, he always left his lights on in his rooms on election days.

Blakely was a strange town with its own unique character. The black folks were poor but beautiful in their own way. Fact was they were so poverty stricken in those depression days and their housing so sorry that their clothing and bedding would get wet most times it rained. It was nothing to see them putting out their clothing and bedding the next day to dry in the sun.

Everybody in the town was a member of one big family, related by blood or marriage. Again, we stuck to our world and the whites to theirs. In Blakely, my biggest resentment against the whites was the way they treated us in the local clothing store.

The folks had set ideas about what black folks should wear. Once you walked into the store the clerk showed you mostly black or blue dresses and only black stockings. We were just out of college wearing short skirts and three quarter length coats, flanked by long string of beads and hanging earrings. We were looking for high fashion clothing. We had been taught in college that black people could wear all colors and hues of the rainbow. At Paine College, we had a home economic teacher who selected colors and had us to model before the class. We just were not going to settle for what the folks in this town wanted us to do. Our dresses were colorful and neatly fitted.

I went in one time, and the saleslady asked whether I was going to buy a dress I was admiring.

"I don't know," I said, "it depends on whether it fits or not."

Well, she just looked at me and said, "You know we don't allow coloreds to try on dresses. You try it on in this store, and you have to buy it."

I was in the store with three other young teachers, and when we heard what the saleslady had to say, we walked out of the store together. We decided that if we couldn't try on the store's dresses like the white women, then we'd buy our clothes by mail order. The store had a very poor selection anyway, carrying for example, only white or black stockings and little in the way of stylish dresses.

Almost immediately, we began to go to Dothan, Alabama, every pay day to make such purchases. We also began to order clothing through the big Three Sisters Department Store in Atlanta. These people offered a wide selection of everything young women could want in the way of stylish wear, even in stockings.

Soon we noticed that our mail ordered packages were being tampered with before delivery. We suspected someone at the local Post Office was peeking into them to see what we had ordered. They must've told the Blakely clothing store because we began to get letters soliciting our business—even informing us that we could try on the dresses without being obligated to buy them, but they still wouldn't let other black women do the same so we stayed away from the store.

Our boycott served in a small way to break down another barrier as did the way we walked outside and left the lights burning on election day. Other blacks began to follow our example and stopped being so intimidated all the time. Still, there was that other world that would just sort of let you come in a little bit. Like you can spend your money, black folks, but don't get any ideas that you can stay.

No, we fought discrimination and segregation as much as we could in our own little ways. We fought them as much as we could without asking to get our heads broken. We didn't go out and about saying we were going to pick a fight. No way then we could've won, but we never accepted segregation. Never. We lived with it, but we didn't accept it.

The main thing about the South then was that you had the whites and blacks and the mulattoes in between, and they all knew what was going on in each other's world. You take the blacks working in the white man's kitchen, and you knew they weren't going to be too hard on those people. No way they were going to lose or maim those people they wanted to come and cook for them and do so many other tasks.

And you have to remember, there are a lot of people of mixed blood, and no white man—even if he's a member of the Ku Klux Klan—is going to hurt any black child or young man he knows is his blood. I remember one night early on at Blakely how I told a black youth how scared I was of the KKK. I told him I was thinking of leaving but couldn't because I needed the job. I had to work.

He said I shouldn't worry. No white man would hurt me. His father was a big man. "My daddy owns all this land."

I just looked at him like he was crazy. "Your daddy?" And he responded that his father also owned the town drugstore.

I said I didn't believe a black man could own that much property. He said, "My daddy isn't a black man. He's as white as they come."

His daddy not only owned the land and the drugstore, but he was also the white leader in town. Until then, I had considered the white man to be of low character and have little possessions. But, in fact, he was "Mr. It" in the area of Blakely. Such white men in the South usually had two families. They had a black family, and they had a white family. And you could say what you want, but they usually took very good care in a secretive way of their black family.

Chapter 12

A Rewarding Year

DURING MY FIRST YEAR OF TEACHING in Blakely, I heard that an old boyfriend was living one county over and dropped him a note. Shortly, our old friendship was renewed as the love letters flew back and forth. I urged him to visit.

When he finally came by, I noticed that one of my roommates couldn't take her eyes off him. She even made it a point to talk to him and be around to say goodbye when he was leaving. After his visit, his letters seldom came any longer. When I inquired about the reason, he always had some excuse or another.

About that time, this roommate began to insist on going to the Post Office for the mail. Simultaneously, she began talking about a new boyfriend—a secretive type who never came around. I noticed, though, that many of the things she said about him fitted my friend. For example, she said he didn't like girls to wear makeup. I remember when I used to get upset with him at Paine College, I would go into the rest room and apply lipstick and rouge liberally and then go out and sit directly in front of him. He'd get so angry that he'd just leave.

She mentioned that he was an artist of sort, and I knew well that my friend had been the school artist at Paine. Anytime art work or decorations or charts or signs were needed, he would accept the project. He also had beautiful penmanship. His drawings were superb.

My classroom was always a great attraction because of the drawings he gave me to decorate it. One particular drawing I have always remembered. It was done to illustrate the poem "Trees" by Joyce Kilmer, who had been killed in the war in the year I was born. It was a lovely spring scene with a budding tree in the center, a nest of robins atop a branch, and the earth springing to life underneath.

Sometimes, when he was happy, he would sketch me and discreetly slip the sketch to me when he thought no one was looking. He sketched me repeatedly, and I had a drawer full of them. Usually he would do it in the school library where we had to keep silent. However, we found other ways to communicate.

Anyway, I finally got suspicious of my roommate and took to racing her to the Post Office for our mail. Sure as sin, there he was writing letters to her. I'd know his meticulous handwriting anywhere. I also poked about and found out that my roommate had been to visit him in the next county.

Boy, was I angry. I quickly packed up all his letters and sent them off to him and demanded that he send back all of mine. In response, he mailed me this magnificent romantic drawing in which he expressed his great love for me. He also used the big drawing to sketch out some of the precious memories we shared and to predict our future together. He just never gave up.

He was wasting his time. I never acknowledged his new letters. I also never mentioned one word about him to my roommate. She must've been waiting anxiously for me to berate her, but I acted like he didn't exist. He was just another love that I absolutely turned off for his betrayal of our relationship.

Later, I heard that my roommate asked Mrs. Swett whether I had told her about the letters. The landlady told her that I had and that I also knew about her correspondence with my artistic "friend," about their visits back and forth, and about my roommate bragging that she had taken him away from me. Unfortunately, once I quit him, he lost his attraction for my roommate. Seems she wasn't as glamorous after all as she thought. In my mind, he was just trying to show how popular he could be with the ladies. She never had the nerve to bring him up again in my hearing.

All the time during my first year out of college, I was developing this great love of teaching. Part of it was the salary, of course, but it was also the respect the parents and children showed us. Then there was a sense of truly giving the young kids skills and tools that could help them as adults and of being rewarded by their interest and joy when they got to understand what you were trying to teach them.

Along about that time, I also began to develop my philosophy of teaching—teaching as if the woods are on fire. Have you ever seen an extensive wood fire? One where the flames roar through the trees and brush and burn for days over a great area of land? I sort of would see myself as a fireman who would never dream of quitting but just goes on battling to overcome the blaze that was seeking to destroy knowledge.

As a teacher, I felt that I could never stop trying to enlighten the children. There were so many children who were sadly ignorant of even basic knowledge to survive in the world. There was so much to be done in the way of teaching them to cope.

Where we lived as a child, I saw numerous wood fires. Many of them you couldn't put out with just water but had to dig open spaces and hope the flames wouldn't leap over them; or try to set back fires that would confront the main blaze, and they'd burn each other out. With all those dry piny woods, we had some terrible fires.

So, I came to see that I had to teach as if the woods were on fire to douse the flames of ignorance, apathy, and depression before they wiped out my classroom. To teach to put out ignorance is how I thought about it. The fires were never going to be totally extinguished, but at least you had to do your share to fight them if many of the children were to be saved.

At Blakely, we worked diligently to teach our children, and their parents loved us in return. On Sunday, there were always invitations for all of us to go to various homes for dinner. Some parents even baked hot rolls and sent them to us for breakfast. Others washed and ironed our clothes and came to the house to clean our rooms.

In March of 1940, when the war in Europe was also in its first year and America was still minding its own business, we received these official letters informing us that the State of Georgia was unable to pay its teachers. Can you imagine that? They were only paying us 55 dollars a month, and they couldn't pay even that small sum.

Mr. King, the education chairman, called a meeting to decide what to do. Did we continue to work without pay and hope for the best or did we call it a day and go home to wherever? The school trustees and church folks offered to provide free room and board if we stayed. Finally, we decided to postpone our decision for the weekend and accept a standing invitation to visit Tuskegee Institute across the border in Alabama. We promised to give our answer when we returned.

We drove to Tuskegee in several cars through a drizzling rain and were warmly welcomed by a group of officials and professors. One of the first places we visited on campus was the laboratory of Dr. George Washington Carver, the famous black agricultural chemist, who discovered so many uses for peanuts, soybeans, and sweet potatoes. Luck was with us since Dr. Carver was in his lab—although we were not allowed to enter.

A guide told us, however, to be patient because in about 10 minutes, he would leave his lab to go to lunch, and we would see him pass by on the walkway. Sure enough—as we stood in the soft rain—a spare frail man came out of the lab and walked toward us deep in thought. Still, he took a few moments as he passed by to respond warmly to our greetings and words of praise. It was a great thrill for us to see such a noted black man whose work was known worldwide. Three years later he would be dead.

While at Tuskegee, we also visited the beautiful chapel and listened to the school's excellent choir. As I listened, I felt a spirit of both giving and living possessing my mind and soul. We sat in hushed silence and let the beautiful music soothe our thoughts.

We had little to say on our return trip, filled as our minds were about our visit to Tuskegee and meeting Dr. Carver and our decision about teaching without pay. Back in Blakely, we went almost immediately to the faculty room to meet with Mr. King, other officials, and townspeople. You could feel the tension in the air as everybody awaited our decision. First, though, the pastor prayed and asked that the Lord help his people to accept our decision—no matter what it was.

Then Mr. King asked that we speak briefly about our experiences at Tuskegee. It all seemed a bit odd as though everyone was putting off the moment when we would announce our decision. When we announced finally that we had decided to stay on and teach without any salary, it seemed almost anticlimactic by then. Not to the townspeople. Their applause and hurrahs rocked the room like booming thunder.

Right off, on Monday morning, the parents began doing their best to show their appreciation to us. A file of children brought us bags of pecans, peanuts, and potatoes. One brought her offerings in a pillow case because there was no paper bag handy. I emptied the pillow case and gave it to the child who returned week after week with gifts of food.

In that period, we ate pecans and goobers, as we called peanuts then, day in and day out, and I began to put on weight. Fact is, I've been a fatty ever since then. We got so much food that we began to stockpile it to take home on our vacation days. The parents also provided us with a weekly schedule that told us where we were to have dinner after school each day.

Those were truly wonderful days, rewarding days. Such hospitality, such appreciative adults. Such beautiful children of every hue, resembling lovely floral bouquets.

That year in Blakely was the most enjoyable and rewarding year in my teaching career. Our feeling was that we couldn't be fired because we hadn't been hired, in effect, since we were not drawing any salary. As a result, we felt no pressure from the authorities and received no complaints from the trustees and parents. We were free to teach at our pace, and I further developed my philosophy of teaching as if the woods were on fire. In such an unrestrictive environment, we all felt compelled to give teaching our very best.

It was truly a golden period. We felt good about ourselves. We were college graduates who knew how to dress stylishly, maybe too much for the local folks taste. We were treated as adults. Our opinions were respected. The hospitality was great, and we were well fed.

It was in that period that I learned you didn't need a lot of money to be happy and to make others happy. I was happy just being able to teach for free. It was a most rewarding feeling.

All too soon, the school year at Blakely came to a close. We had a memorable graduation exercise. I was very moved by it, seeing so many students praised and promoted. We had won the hearts of the people which they openly acknowledged during the ceremonies. I went home to Augusta with a heart that was happy and fulfilled, but I was never to return to Blakely.

Chapter 13

A Dishonored Student

I RETURNED HOME IN THE EARLY SUMMER OF 1940 with the war in Europe going badly for the Allies. France and the low countries had fallen to the German army, and everybody wondered how long England could survive alone. Folks talked without letup about whether America would get into it and listened to President Roosevelt tell us on the radio that no American boys would die in another European war.

With newly opened Fort Gordon nearby and all the soldiers everywhere in town, we had constant reminders of the military and what use it might be put to. Lucky me, I got a job as a clerk at the fort for the summer and loved it. There were so many fellows looking for a date, and I had so many opportunities to go dancing at the encampment or at US0-type facilities for the black soldiers in Augusta.

As September approached, I wanted to continue working at Fort Gordon, but my mama, as always, insisted that she had sent me to school so I could teach. In any case, my application for work at a school in Sylvania had been accepted so I packed up and went by bus the 50 miles to Sylvania in Screven County south of Augusta.

Unlike Blakely, where I had taught the lower grades in elementary school, I was assigned to teach science and history to high school students. Imagine my surprise when I found that some of my new students could hardly read or write, at all. How in the world had they ever gotten promoted to high school? It was very discouraging working with them, and I yearned many times to go back to teaching first and second graders. At least with them, I could concentrate on teaching them to read.

Outside of school, I really had fun because the town barber—who was handsome but a lot older—took a fancy to me. Seems that every new school year, he'd look the new young teachers over and choose one to be sort of his girlfriend. I became his choice that year because I was the youngest teacher and the most talkative.

He was a good-looking man with a great sense of humor, and best of all he owned a new car and was a sport about driving you about and taking you to concerts in the surrounding towns. I'll always remember our first picnic before Easter when he organized the whole thing for a bunch of us. We even got the home economics teacher to make all kinds of goodies and contribute baked chicken and ribs.

The barber had picked a site way out in the woods for the picnic which went on until late into the night. At one point, I told him that I was scared and wanted to go home for fear the sheriff would catch us and I'd lose my job. The barber surprised me by revealing that the father of his friend, John, was the law and had bought the land we were playing on for him. I thought he was pulling my leg, but I found out later that John's father was indeed a powerful white man who owned a big part of the property in Sylvania, including the main grocery store and would do anything for any of John's friends.

John never talked openly about his father, but he knew who he was. In turn, the father did whatever possible for his black son and his black friends.

I quickly learned that the black folks in Sylvania were hospitable and friendly if you didn't put on airs and act superior. You especially weren't expected to impress your superiors or cozy up to them as a way to keep your job. In time, I learned to relax and be myself and enjoy the town and the people. It also gave me a warm feeling to know that there were white people in high places who had a familiar interest in us and would look out for us.

On Saturdays, a group of young teachers would dress up and go up to town and watch the local folks walk slowly around the commercial blocks. We thought it was amusing to see how they moved at a snail's pace. Curious, I asked my landlady one day why everybody in town walked so slowly. I had to add the snippy observation that I thought "it looked silly."

She looked at me in a bemused way and said, "Well, we think some of the things you new teachers do is silly. You rush to get to town and circle the block in three or four minutes, and then you don't know what to do with yourselves. You all wind up standing around or sitting in your cars. That's pretty silly to us."

I gave some thought to her comments and finally had to agree with her. You just never know how others see you. Certainly not as we see ourselves or imagine how they see us.

Things became a little involved when I saw more and more of the barber. A woman sent me word through the local channels that he would never marry me or anyone else. That didn't bother me because I had no intention of getting married to him. She went on to confide she had a baby by him, and he knew that she would kill him if he ever did marry anyone else.

Then another friend who was married to an older man invited me to supper and wasted no time in providing me with the latest gossip. She took time out to emphasize that I should never marry an older man. She went on to say that her husband had died years before and left her with two children and a big farm. Out of a desire to survive, she had married another older man who had a mule and plow and could work the land. Later, they had moved into town, and she had remained with him out of respect but felt she had missed much in the way of fun and excitement in not marrying a younger man.

I got another message about my barber friend from one of his cousins who invited all the teachers to her house on a Saturday night for a chitterling and rice bash. She went out of her way to explain to me how her cousin, the barber, fixed himself up with a new teacher every year. It would be best, she suggested, if I didn't get too serious about him. Well, I had no intention of getting serious, but he was a lot of fun and a good sport, and I just decided to enjoy myself in his company during my first year in Sylvania.

What I heard about him was mostly right. When I returned for my second year, he was up to his old trick of finding himself a new teacher to squire around town. He thought he could date her and still see me—hang onto us both by keeping us from knowing about the other. Well, Sylvania was too small to try that act, and I quickly turned off my feelings for him—permanently.

Another thing I remember is that the Board of Education required all applicants for a teaching job to include a photograph of themselves. One of the applicants who was accepted was very light, and the white superintendent mistakenly assigned her to a white school. However, upon meeting her at the train station, he realized his error and was highly embarrassed. His solution was to contact the barber and have him find her a place to stay. Overnight, she became one of his girlfriends.

But that wasn't the end of the matter. Because of their embarrassment, the superintendent and the members of the black Board of Education arranged for her to teach in the black high school and even offered to create a supervisory job for her. What they feared most was that she would file a suit for breach of contract because she had been offered a job at a white school and room and board with a white family. Unhappily, she was too white to be black and not white enough to be white. Can you follow that?

I was really beginning to enjoy teaching that year since the kids were so eager to learn so many things. One particularly bright spot in the class was a girl named Jane. She was short, fat, and dark with the most beautiful smile I'd ever seen. She was so eager to learn that it just inspired me to try to be the best teacher possible.

She often consoled me when I became discouraged because some of the children couldn't or wouldn't learn. Jane would look directly at me and say, "Remember, many of us appreciate your teaching. We'll make it with your help."

I'd cheer up again and give her a big smile. Then she'd go back to her school work. She was so quiet and worked so diligently—I just had to reach for the stars.

When graduation time approached, we set about to find the students best suited to be the class valedictorian and salutorian. The grades were tallied informally, and to my delight, Jane appeared to be the top honor student. I was so happy and thrilled for her, but it wasn't meant to be.

No sooner had the news leaked out that she probably was that year's top student than the gossip started. It began in part when one mother telephoned to say that Jane's selection as valedictorian would disgrace the whole school. She would not tell me why, though.

I summoned Jane and asked her what the woman could've meant by her comment. I'll always remember that Jane came over to my big chair, leaned her head in my lap, and cried. Shortly she stopped and told me the following story.

It went back to when Jane's older sister was in the hospital having her sixth baby, and her mother sent her to cook for the sister's husband and five children. She never really liked her brother-in-law—especially the way he leered at her—and she always left the dining room once she had placed the food on the table. No matter, he kept sneaking around to be alone with her and trying to get her to take a drink of moonshine liquor which she never touched.

One night about 2 a.m., he tiptoed into her bedroom while she was asleep and raped her, stifling her cries for help with his hands. He warned her to be silent or she'd wake the children, and they would see them together in the bed. She said the harder she fought him the more he raped her.

She never said a word afterward. She was scared to tell her mother because they were such a close family. She never told her sister about it either when she came home from the hospital with an infant girl.

Three months later, though, the mother suspected something was wrong because her daughter had become withdrawn and moody. She confronted her, and Jane told her the whole story. By then, she knew she was pregnant and was going to have the brother-in-law's baby.

In tears, she asked her mother what could she do? Should she tell her sister? Should she go away so as not to disgrace the family?

The mother and daughter cried for awhile before the mother cautioned her not to say anything to her sister or her husband. She noted that he was a mean man and could be cruel to her sister who had to stay with him because of the six children. Where would her sister ever be able to find work and be able to feed her children?

The mother had to leave for work in Dr. Carleton's office, and he soon learned what was going on when he found the mother crying to herself on her lunch break. He soothed her and made an appointment for Jane. After examining her, the physician provided her with medicine that she was to take at home. Soon she was not pregnant any more.

It was another black lady who worked in Dr. Carleton's

office who had called me and began the gossip about Jane. It was not clear how she had found out. Jane's mother and Dr. Carleton never told her. We surmised that he must have recorded the matter in some way, and she came across it. It turned out that her daughter was also a contender for top honors that year.

At the end of her story, Jane told me that she was determined to go to Savannah State College. It seemed there was another sister there who could help her with room and board. Somehow she would get by and obtain her degree.

I asked Jane to bring her mother around so I could talk to her about this situation. The mother begged me not to stir up a hornet's nest for Jane by giving her high marks. "Miss Burton, I only hope you will help me get my daughter into college. Let that woman's daughter get first honors and someone else second."

She went on to explain that she just wanted Jane to have the chance to succeed. "She's a good girl, and I've always believed her account of the rape, but we can't tell her sister. It would break her heart, and she can't leave her husband because she's got the children. For the same reason, we can't take my son-in-law to court."

There was a lot more discussion, and in the end, I promised I would do what I could to make sure Jane wasn't named the top student. With great sadness and reluctance, I jiggled her grades to pull her average down. When the formal vote was taken, my fellow teachers became angry that Jane's marks in my classes had thwarted their efforts to select her as valedictorian. I quickly forgot their reaction, however, when I saw the smile on Jane's face.

Some six years later, I was attending a teachers gathering in Savannah when I noticed a slim young lady pulling a male teacher toward me. To my amazement, I realized it was Jane. How confident, happy, and stylish she looked.

She hugged me affectionately and said, "John, this lovely lady is the cause of it all. I will always be so grateful to her. You remember me explaining my plight before we married. This is the lady who gave me a new life." John joined in hugging me, and I hugged them both.

Jane has never been out of my mind since then. It gives me such a warm glow to know she made something of herself after such a traumatic experience and that I had a hand in it. In those days, if it had come out that she was pregnant, she would have been expelled from school and church. I also could have been in jeopardy for not reporting her abortion.

Chapter 14

The Good War

DURING THE SUMMER OF 1941, I worked again at Fort Gordon. The pay was better than what I made as a teacher, but mama still insisted that I return to Sylvania to teach in the fall. It was my third year as a professional teacher, and I was far more confident than I had been that initial year in Blakely. I continued to teach as if the woods were on fire—fire being ignorance, indifference, and stupidity—and I had to fight them like I was fighting a blazing forest fire.

We were all shocked on a quiet Sunday in December when the radio announced that the Japanese had attacked Pearl Harbor in the Hawaiian Islands. A lot of Americans were killed and wounded, and President Roosevelt wasted no time in declaring war against them. We thought that the Japanese had to be crazy to try to fight us with their canvas-covered airplanes and that the United States would whip them in just a few weeks.

I remember sitting in the corner store sipping a soda through a straw and wondering whether Georgia would be bombed next. At school the next day, we had the children practice air raid drills and instructed them to get their parents to black out their homes so no light would show and let the enemy know where Sylvania was located. Fact is, some parents came to school early to collect their children and take them home in a hurry.

Of course, the Japanese never bombed Georgia. No way their planes could reach it. But those were exciting scary days as the country and the people geared up to fight the Japanese. Next thing we knew, the Germans under Hitler decided to help Japan fight us and then we had a war in the Pacific and another one in Europe. Very soon, many of the young men we knew had volunteered for one or another branch of the service and gone off to fight. Mama wrote that Augusta was overflowing with troops training at Fort Gordon, and everybody had work and good pay.

We didn't truly suffer a lot during the war. We were mostly aware of it because of all the servicemen in uniform, the newspaper stories and photos, the newsreels at the movie houses, the word of some relative or friend killed in battle, and the rationing that went on at home. Sugar and butter, gasoline and tires were among the rationed items. Everybody got a ration book which allowed you so much meat, butter, and sugar a month. They had stickers, too, for the car windshields which told how much gasoline you were allowed.

It seems like we were always filling out one form or another and that someone was asking your birthday, the color of your eyes and hair, and where you were born. And we were always filling out one form or another for the students. The children were very hard to teach in those war years because their fathers and brothers, uncles and aunts were in the service. Now and then, a child would be absent for several days to attend a funeral or a memorial service.

I heard after the war that more than 320,000 men and women from Georgia served during the war. Almost 7,000 of them were killed or wounded. The state legislature voted to drop the legal age to vote from 21 to 18—not that it affected my people in any way. The thinking was if you could fight for your country at 18, you could vote for its leaders.

Early on in the war, Ellis Arnall, a former attorney general for the state, defeated old Gene Talmadge and became the governor. The big issue between them was not segregation for a change but the issue of academic freedom—freeing up the schools from political influence. Governor Arnall moved swiftly to get the legislature to approve a law which removed the governor from the Board of Regents of the University of Georgia. No longer would governors like old Gene be able to stack the board with his cronies.

The war was sad for all the unhappiness it brought to so many families, but it was also good for many people because of the work it provided. There was work for all who wanted it—black and white. Cotton was king again in the South because of the demand for it by the military services. Among the cotton-growing states, Georgia ranked fifth, by 1943. At the same time, though, the state was first in the production of sweet potatoes, peanuts, pecans, watermelons, velvet beans, and pimento peppers. Old farms were turned into productive acreage.

So I spent the war teaching at the high school in Sylvania and working summers at Fort Gordon. Despite the war and the unhappiness it caused for many, it was a good time to be young and alive. My favorite pastime continued to be dancing. The big band music was unforgettable. We also broke up the two-step dance sets with jitterbug numbers. I danced every chance I got away from work and homework whether during the school year or at home during the summers.

One war year after another passed, and soon we could see America was going to win against the Japanese and the Germans. It was about then that one of my old Paine College boyfriends, the artist who had contacted me in Sylvania, wormed his way back into my life. He began by writing me these very endearing letters asking for my forgiveness for his past behavior. Reluctantly, at first, I responded with letters of my own, and soon we had a lively correspondence flowing.

He was a charmer, no doubt of that. Of course, I had a big crush on him before so I guess I loosened the spigot a little bit and let him gradually back into my life. All too soon we not only were dating, but we became engaged. He was in Augusta then, and I was in Sylvania. By mail, we moved quickly to get our wedding plans into motion. All so quickly, he had rented a house that we could buy if I liked it. I hadn't seen the house because of my work schedule and told him to just rent it for now. One thing I learned from mama was to watch my pennies and not make any extravagant purchases without careful planning. In other words, don t buy a car unless you have a place to park it.

Next thing I knew, he had set a date for me to meet with him and select the furniture. Within a day or so, he phoned to tell me that his mother had selected the furniture and that we would have to pay for it as agreed upon. I was very unhappy about that. After mulling it over for several days, I wrote to inform him I would be the one to select the furniture for us after I went up to Augusta. No way was I going to let his mother interfere with us right from the beginning.

Well, I didn't hear from him for a spell, and then I got a letter from him. He announced that if I had a problem with his mother, I could forget about the wedding. Still, he said he hoped I would bend to his mother's choice of furniture and come and live with her while he was away in the army.

I was taken aback by how determined he was to let his mother make so many decisions for us and how easily he could put aside our wedding plans. I must say I also had no idea at all that he was about to be drafted into the service to fight in the war. Why had he waited until then to tell me?

The biggest surprise of all, though, was the fact that after posting this letter, he tried to prevent the post office people from delivering it. He called his local post office and mine and even sent telegrams beseeching them not to deliver his letter to me. Unaware, I no sooner had received the letter than the mailman was at the door requesting that I give it back to him. I told him that he had no right to make such a request and that I was not about to grant his demand. Anyway, I said, I had already opened it.

So I read the letter over and over again and decided that my artist friend was definitely not for me. He was no good before, and he was no good again. To make it worse, he obviously was a mama's boy, and I'd get nothing but grief from both of them. Maybe it was a good thing he was going in the army. Maybe they'd get him to snap his strings to mama's apron and make a man of him.

I sat down finally and wrote him a heart-to-heart letter to tell him that he was as much a conniving rascal as ever and I wouldn't marry him if I was stuck with only him on an island forever. I berated him for permitting his mother to interfere and for not informing me about his draft status. I told him that I would rather remain with my mama, a loving and concerned mama, and care for her in her old age than marry anyone like him.

About ten years later, I saw the postman who had tried to retrieve the letter. He inquired whether I could tell him what was in the letter to make the writer so desperate to stop its delivery. I simply thanked him for delivering the letter and pointed out, "It changed my whole life. I met a wonderful man and now am happily married and have a wonderful son."

Chapter 15

Marriage and Motherhood

THE LONG WAR CAME TO AN END IN 1945, and we all celebrated V-E Day and then V-J Day and went on with our lives. The GIs came home, and the blacks among them thought things would be a lot better for us because of their contributions to the war effort. Well, nothing had changed after they fought in World War I, and nothing was about to change, at least drastically, after World War II. Live and learn.

I continued to travel back and forth between Augusta and Sylvania and to work summers at Fort Gordon. Mama was getting on, and there was no one at home with her. I thought I should look for a teacher's job in Augusta, but mama said she didn't want me shaking up my life for her sake.

Gene Talmadge ran again for governor in 1946, stirring up the old fears the white man bore the black man in Georgia. Once again, race was his issue. In March, 1946, the white primary election, which had kept the black folks from voting, was ruled illegal by a federal court. Talmadge railed that blacks would soon be skedaddling to the polls looking for a ballot to mark. Where might that lead, he thundered?

Well, old Gene won the primary on the issue and went

on to win the November general election. But fate intervened, and he died before he was inaugurated. A rigged write-in vote then brought of all people—his son, Herman—into office. But the vote was challenged, and the state high court said Mel Thompson, the lieutenant governor, was the rightful successor to Gene Talmadge.

Amidst all this sound and fury, most black folks just went on about their business in their black world. Only a few of us considered trying to register to vote in light of the federal court decision but didn't put thought to action. Georgia and Mississippi still were the collective lynching capital of the world. Realistically, it was still a case of discretion being the better part of valor. We felt that our day would come, but not then.

One summer during the war, while working again at Fort Gordon, I met a tall handsome soldier named George Crawford. He was olive-colored and quite slim, and I was almost instantly smitten. He courted me all that summer and wrote faithfully when I returned to teaching in Sylvania in the fall. When I had a free weekend or he had a weekend pass or a furlough, we'd spent every moment possible together.

When school ended the following June, I came home, and we married in August. Neither of us had very much money so we had a quiet wedding at my home with the military chaplain officiating. Mama insisted that we live with her although George still had to spend most of his time on the post.

September came and my husband asked me not to return to my teaching job in Sylvania. I readily agreed to stay home and continued working at Fort Gordon. In November, since I was then pregnant, George insisted that I leave work and stay at home and take care of myself. He had his soldier's pay and an allotment for me.

We were very happy in those few hours or days when he was allowed off the post, but within several months, he was sent to officer's candidate school and then to Fort Huacahua in Arizona. Except for some visits to see him at Fort Benning, I remained home with mama. George thought I'd be better off in my condition to remain with her rather than join him in the desert, out West.

George had a lovely aunt named Ethel, who wrote to tell me how happy she was to hear that we were expecting. He was her favorite nephew, and she couldn't do enough for us. Every week or so, she would send me a hand-sewn maternity dress or some article she had made for the baby.

Aunt Ethel also wrote to say she wanted George and me to visit her as soon as possible after the baby was born. Strangely, she never sent a photograph of herself, but that mystery was solved when she revealed to me that she was passing as white in her town. She kept two houses and provided the address of the one in the colored section where she asked that we meet.

Frankly, I was perturbed and hurt by this revelation and found it difficult to write Ethel for some time. Eventually, she wrote me a lengthy letter to explain why she was passing for white. The gist of it was that white widows were entitled to a lot of free things and didn't have to pay taxes.

I accepted her explanation, and shortly she sent me several photographs of herself. She was very beautiful and quite elegant. In several of them, she could be seen carrying a flag in some parade. Others showed her with various rich boyfriends.

When Ethel died, George and I went to the law office for the reading of her will. Her lawyer almost had a heart attack and began to sweat profusely when he saw my husband and I were black. In fact, he jumped up and ran out of his office and shortly sent in his secretary to query us about Ethel. We proved eventually that Ethel indeed was black which meant that the white lawyer—among other white men—had been dating a black woman for years.

Mama was very pleased that George's folks were genuinely concerned about us and looked forward to the birth of the baby. I think, too, she was happy I was pregnant because it kept me from accompanying George from camp to camp. Not that I blamed mama since she was alone at home now except for me, and in failing health.

My, my, how exciting it was to be rushed to the Fort Gordon hospital late on a Saturday night. I was so naive about such things that I didn't realize women had labor pains before giving birth. The army was still segregated then, and they had to give me a private room because I was the only black patient. Still, I couldn't get over how attentive and kind all the personnel were to me.

Our bundle of joy, also to be named George, arrived early on Sunday. It was Mother's Day, May 12, 1943. I thought of my husband and how much he wanted a son and how much he would want to be there.

I remained in the hospital seven days without putting even my feet on the floor. Not like today where you have the baby, and you're out the door the next day. The nurses couldn't do enough for little George whom they nicknamed "Chocolate Drop" because there were few black infants born at Fort Gordon.

My husband George was given leave and flew home from Arizona. When he arrived to take us home, I noted the open admiration for my tall handsome soldier. I was so happy and proud that he was all mine and that we now had a son to share our love.

The days of his furlough passed swiftly. Each was a joy to be savored and stored up in our treasury of memories. George took the greatest pride and happiness in holding his son at every opportunity. All too soon, though, it was time for him to return to Arizona. We parted tearfully with his planning for me to join him in September.

Well, one thing led to another, and I didn't get to join him as he had hoped. In all honesty, I was not crazy about the idea of taking the baby out to Arizona to live and to be alone on the hot dusty post for days on end while George was out tramping around in the field. I imagined all kinds of terrible things happening to my son in the form of strange desert illnesses and fevers and constantly saw images of poisonous snakes and spiders circling his crib.

In truth, too, I missed teaching which I had come to think of as my first love. I missed the challenge of standing before a new class of students and wondering how much I could influence them in the coming school year. I missed the day-to-day excitement of trying to inspire my students to seize the moment and make something of themselves. I missed most of all the great personal satisfaction of teaching as if the woods were on fire.

Living with mama, I came to realize that she was trying in her own way to take control of my baby. Except for letting me fix his formula, she insisted on doing everything for him. I loved my mama and didn't want to get into a personal conflict with her about raising little George, but he was my baby. Still, she was the mother of 14 children and knew a lot more about taking care of them than I did. Fine, I thought. She's getting on, and it makes her very happy so why not? As for myself, maybe I'll go back to teaching.

And I did go back to teaching school, and my husband George continued to pursue his army career. The following year, the Korean War broke out, and he was ordered overseas but sadly became sick on the troop ship. He was taken off and sent back to the States where he lingered for some time with a debilitating disease before passing away at a young age. It was a real tragedy and nearly broke my heart. I was terribly broken up for a while. Finally, though, I got hold of myself for my son's sake and my school children.

It was doubly hard for a young widow in those days not to stoop to the vices readily available to all. Most tempting were all the young men who still were around. Many of them though were just like the boll weevil, chewing the lifeblood out of the cotton crop. So many were just looking for a home and a free ride. Widows of servicemen were a prime target because of the ten thousand dollars we got in insurance from the government.

I recognized that I had a trio of choices. I could become an alcoholic and hide in my house, take up with a man—any man—to ease my loneliness, or go back to teaching. I chose the latter in time.

Still, as a young widow, I was constantly pestered by men, single and married. I quickly learned a number of ways to put them off. One way was for me to keep my hat and car keys near the door, and when the doorbell rang, to scoop them up and tell the caller I was just on my way out the door. If I wasn't dressed to go out, I would place the vacuum cleaner in the middle of the floor and turn it on with the arrival of an unwanted caller, telling him I was busy and couldn't talk. Sometimes, I'd just call my next door neighbor and invite her over for a cup of tea or to see a new dress. The caller would weary of female talk and soon leave.

One of my callers was a married preacher who claimed that the Lord had sent him to me because I had a house in which we could have sex discreetly. His wife was sick, he explained, and I was just the ticket to fill in for her. In doing so, he would maintain his respectability.

I suggested that he return to his home and ask the devil for further guidance. I made it very clear to him that I had no intention of dating any married man.

Back at home with mama, I just got up early one morning, dressed, and informed mama that I was going to get a job. I could see that my announcement made her happy—mostly because she would get to take care of the baby all day. With that settled, I went off to see the superintendent of schools to apply for a job.

Getting an appointment, I was reminded by him, 'You know the law. We do not hire married teachers in

Richmond County, and we do not let married teachers teach in Richmond County."

That seemed to be the end of our discussion, but then he added, "I have one principal who is difficult to please, and we'll see how you work out with him as a substitute teacher. Coincidentally, one of his teachers just married, and he had to dismiss her."

The principal was a very intelligent man who had passed an examination for postmaster with the highest mark. Seems he was told that there was no place for a black man as postmaster. As an appeasement, he was given a school administration job and quickly became qualified to be a school principal. In that post, he could pick his own teachers and happily picked me to be a substitute teacher for 29 days—the longest term possible for a substitute.

I noticed in that period that he kept his office door opened so he could listen to me teach my class—especially the citizenship course. After I had to stop my substitute work, he interviewed a number of other candidates for the opening but declined to accept any of them. He insisted that none of them truly knew how to teach.

To resolve the impasse, the superintendent asked the principal to tell him exactly the kind of teacher he wanted and needed. The principal said that he wanted a certified four-year teacher with solid teaching experience, a description I easily filled.

Shortly, I was contacted and offered a job as a permanent substitute. You might say I was the first married teacher hired to work in Richmond County. While I received the same salary as regular teachers, I was not granted any benefits. After one year in the job, I wrote to the school board and asked to become a full-time teacher with all the benefits.

Very quickly I was summoned to the office of the superintendent who asked, "You get the same pay as the other teachers, so why aren't you satisfied?" I informed him that

I had an offer in Boston for a permanent job and did not want to turn it down for one that had no security or benefits.

He noted that I was the only teacher capable of satisfying the professional standards of the school principal so I must have been a good teacher. He said, "You go out there and teach for him, and I'll talk with the board."

The next year, the board changed the law, and my job became permanent. Thereafter, teachers did not have to resign if they got married. Once more, I felt like I was teaching as if the woods were on fire.

I was happy about the change, but there were some folks who were not happy that I was allowed to teach even though married. I remember two old maids saying to my face that someone should report me for being married. I just smiled and informed them the superintendent was well aware that I was married, and they should also know that I had a son. Other gossips contacted my friends to verify that I was even married. One of them was nosy enough to go to the courthouse to look up my marriage license. People sure are funny.

Chapter 16

New School Ventures

IT WAS A VERY EXCITING ERA for a black woman to be teaching in Georgia. President Harry Truman had proposed an extensive new civil rights program in 1948 to give blacks equal job opportunities. Herman Talmadge, who had won the governorship in 1948, and again two years later, was bitterly opposed to anything to do with desegregation and swore he would maintain segregation — especially in Georgia's schools.

He and his followers were shocked in 1954, when the U.S. Supreme Court held that segregation, wherever it existed, had to end "with all deliberate speed." Still, the white diehards managed to keep the schools, including the University of Georgia, segregated until January, 1961. Token integration followed until finally all the schools were integrated in a few years. By then, I had been teaching almost 25 years and could hardly believe the changes that had come about in that period, but it was a most happy day.

As for Richmond County, it didn't actively begin to integrate its schools until 1963, when a case was filed in court, Acree versus the Board of Education. Initially, the county had attempted to oppose integration by various processes including school choice, improvement of black schools, separate but equal schools, and faculty integration, but with a ruling in favor of Acree against the backdrop of favorable federal legislation for almost a decade, desegregation reluctantly was implemented by Richmond County.

When I had gone back to teaching, it was at the Steed Street School, which was a sorry excuse for a schoolhouse. Fact was, it was dilapidated and ready to fall down. Still, I taught there for two years before the authorities decided that it would be cheaper to build a new school than try to renovate the Steed Street one.

While the new school was under construction, classes were held in various churches in the area. Rented space at the Shiloh Orphanage Home was used by the principal and his staff for offices. It was a real make-do situation, and the supply situation was especially bad in those days. We lacked even the most basic tools like pencils and paper.

The principal got to name the school for Ursula Collins, who had been one of his favorite teachers when he was a student. The school was built in the so-called Florida-style, which to my way of thinking left a lot to be desired in the way of space and facilities. Many years later, it was torn down and replaced by a new structure.

I must say that my teaching career at Ursula Collins was both interesting and challenging. A lot of the new ideas in teaching today like reading corners, show and tell, math games, and so on were implemented in those days under different names and with limited funds and resources. For example, one teacher gave her children small milk cartons and had them draw pictures on them to resemble various people's faces. Then they filled them with dirt and planted different types of seeds and tended them while they grew.

I remember that one little boy's seeds never sprouted, and he was quite disappointed. Then his teacher, in a mix of creativity and desperation, told him his carton person was a bald-headed man. The boy seized on that explanation and wrote a prize story called "Baldy."

While at the Ursula Collins School, I came to the conclusion that it would be a good idea to visit the home of every one of my students. I felt that it would help me to understand my students better as well as their many problems. I remember going to one home after school and knocking at the door and being informed by the pupil's mama that "you teachers keep coming here telling me how bad my children are. I'm tired of you all. I do the best I can."

I smiled and said, "Mrs. Hartley, I did not come here to tell you how bad your son has been behaving. Yet, you just told me in a way that he is bad. Why don't we talk about it and see whether we can become friends and work together to help him?"

With that said, Mrs. Hartley invited me in with a shrug of her shoulders and gestured for me to sit on an old dirty sofa stacked with laundry and clutter. I told her that I had come to listen and why didn't she tell me about the children.

She began at once to talk about the three of them, and it was so sad I had to struggle to hold back the tears. She said her son Amos was the worst of the trio, and her husband was determined to break him or kill him. She led me into a back bedroom and pointed to the bloody sheets on which her husband had whipped Amos with his belt.

"He dared me to change the sheets," she said shaking her head. "He whips the kids every day to discipline them. I can't say anything. If I do, he'll beat me, too."

We went back to the front room where Mrs. Hartley begged me to promise not to tell anyone about the beatings—not only of Amos but of the other two children, also. In those days, I knew very little about child abuse and what, if any, laws were involved. Thereafter at school, I showed a very sympathetic side to Amos since I had a vivid awareness of the life he had at home.

I longed, though, to take Mrs. Hartley and the children away from that awful house, but there was just no place to go with them in that time. Shortly, I began trying to give the children the opportunity to be happy at school in an effort to offset somewhat any unhappiness at home. In doing so, I think some of my colleagues began to suspect the unorthodoxy of my teaching methods. So be it.

Indeed, many of my fellow teachers could not understand how I treated the so-called "bad children" so leniently. But I knew and they didn't that many of the children were being either scarred in some way or whipped and slapped about at home. In effect, I pledged to the children that the hours they spent in school would be free of abuse.

Turnabout, some of these abused students—the older ones, of course—abused me in a variety of ways but never physically, lashing out as a sort of way to get back at an adult for what they were experiencing at home. A lot of them would burst into tears when I talked softly to them in an effort to draw them out and get things needed to be said off their chest. I learned the true meaning of patience and reaching out.

I was able over a period of time to get clean clothes for the poorer students and even pay for their hair to be cut. I got the clothes mainly from the Shiloh orphanage which always received more clothing than it could use from well-off folks. With a new outfit and haircut, it was easy to see how the children felt better about themselves. If they looked good, they felt good, is what I figured, and they'll do better in school and maybe things would get better at home for them.

I still have very vivid and pleasant memories of a little black boy named Joey because he was always so well-behaved in class. One day, I asked him to stay after class, and he became upset because he thought he was being punished for something bad he didn't do. Little did he know that I had a very pleasant surprise for him.

You see Joey came from a very poor family, and his

mother was not well. I decided that it was time he had some new clothing and visited the Shiloh Orphanage to pick out two shirts and two pairs of overalls for him. I also got a friend who had a well-paying insurance job and was childless to give me five dollars for a new pair of sneakers. I told him I'd have Joey rake his yard, but he growled that he didn't want any "brats" hanging about his place and to forget it. He was a lovable grouch.

As much as I would've loved to have clothed children like Joey myself, it just wasn't possible. At the time, I was being paid a small monthly salary. Occasionally though, I would buy socks for the boys and ribbons for the little girls.

Joey was delighted when I gave him the clothes and 50 cents for a haircut. I told him to go home and bathe and change his clothes, and I'd come by to take him downtown to buy a new pair of sneakers. When we were finished, I took him home to show him off to his mother. She was all smiles and so appreciative. I left with a happy heart.

The next morning, I looked forward to seeing Joey all dressed up and looking handsome, but alas, he never came to school that day. I was so disappointed and sad that I nearly cried aloud in class.

I asked several children who lived near him if they had seen him. One boy said that Joey had been going around the neighborhood the day before until it was dark. He said he was "all cleaned up and going from house to house."

I told mama about Joey when I got home, and she said some evil spirit must've run off with him to get his new clothes. I prayed and cried but sensed that everything would be back to normal the next morning.

Sure enough, a smiling happy Joey met me at the school door. He sure was a handsome boy, and his clean black skin gleamed like he had just polished it for me. His clothes were still clean although wrinkled a bit.

I gave him a big hug and asked, "Why did you stay out of school yesterday?"

Joey said he was sorry if he had hurt me in any way but was anxious to finish the rounds of his neighborhood to show everyone his new clothes, sneakers, and haircut. "You see, I haven't looked so nice before, and I wanted them to see me. He added that "they all liked the way I looked, but I didn't tell them that you dressed me like this."

I easily understood his concern and assured him that it would be "our secret." Thereafter, whenever he changed his clothes, brushed his hair, and shined his shoes, he'd whisper to me, "our secret," while the other children repeated, "Good morning, Mrs. Crawford."

As I said, some of my colleagues called my methods unorthodox, but I considered them to be a fine way to teach and a good investment in the children for the future.

It was amazing to me how some of the teachers overreacted to some of the things the children did in school. One day, a teacher returned to her room to find a little boy lying on top of a little girl on a table. They were fully dressed and had the class in stitches with the exciting things they were saying to each other.

In a panic, the teacher came running to my room yelling that she was going to take the pair to the principal. I calmed her down and suggested that she let me talk to the children involved. She readily agreed because, as she said, she wouldn't know how to describe the situation to the principal, anyway.

Keeping in mind what I had learned at a series of classes and workshops about such situations, I asked the children, "Where do you live? How many rooms are there in your house? Where do you sleep?"

They were terribly frightened and needed a lot of reassurance that they were not going to be punished before they explained. They lived in a two-room house and slept on the floor at the foot of their parents' bed. The children were neither dumb nor bad. They were only showing their classmates what they had seen at home—an act which many of their little friends could readily relate to.

I asked about their parents and was informed by them that sometimes they fight during the day and play late at night. It was obvious that the children had no genuine clinical knowledge of sexual intercourse involving married adults.

Their teacher agreed with me that somehow or another we had to contact the parents and counsel them about their children's reaction and also counsel the children about keeping home matters at home. We understood that it had to be handled delicately so as not to get the parents upset at the children.

Anyway, teaching at the new school proved to be a very cold experience for several years. The Florida-designed building was very unsuitable to the chilly weather you could experience at times in Georgia. Miami was a long way from Augusta.

When the Bible storyteller came by every day, she'd get so cold that she used her class time to pray for heat. Eventually, we were provided with a space heater, but it was a clunker and blew up on the third day. The children and I were nigh scared to death and ran screaming out of the room.

Next thing, we were sent each day to the lunchroom to study between nine o'clock and 11 a.m. before returning to the cold classroom. I don't know which was worse—the banging of the pots and pans and the loud talk of the kitchen help or the refrigerator we had for our classroom. In the damp chilly winter days, we kept our heavy clothes on all through the school hours. I kept my feet warm by resting them on a heated brick wrapped in paper and cloth.

There were the usual internal politics to contend with as I found at every school where I had taught. At Ursula Collins, you got ahead by worshipping the principal. You were assigned well-behaved children if you spent your extra time hovering around his office to help out in many little ways. Since I was never one to ingratiate myself with anyone in that way, I was given the disinterested and troublesome pupils.

It was okay by me because it just rekindled my determination to teach as if the woods were on fire. I'd tell my new class right off that I loved each and everyone of them, and I hoped they felt or would come to feel the same way about me. They registered genuine surprise that I would speak so openly and take such an approach with them. Many of them obviously had never been told that they were loved and could love in return.

To get them immediately involved, I would say, "Let's make a chart on the blackboard to list the things that we can excel at together this year." Without any assistance from me, they would become increasingly excited and involved as they waved their hands to offer their suggestions. Some of them I remember still—like making every effort to attend school daily, be on time, pick up any rubbish about the grounds, and team up to keep the classroom beautiful.

Considered misfits by other teachers, these classes turned out to be outstanding and with a near perfect attendance record for the year. Even the superintendent finally came by to visit my students to verify all the wonderful things he had been hearing about them and brightened their day by awarding them a certificate of merit. In time, I was voted Ursula Collins teacher of the year and soon afterwards Richmond County teacher of the year.

We garnered so much praise that I was assigned the principal's daughter and groups of excellent children by my third year at the school. Rich or poor, confident or at loose ends, I treated all my children with love and motivated them to raise their self-esteem. Not all of them rated at the top academically, but I insisted that they be well groomed and neatly dressed no matter how old the clothes as I strove to raise the level of their manners overall to 105 percent.

Much though still came down to how you related to the principal. This situation was especially rough on the young female teachers who were beholden to the principal to obtain tenure in their jobs. For his part, he was not above using his position to harm teachers who did not idolize and praise him and, in certain instances, date him.

When he kept asking one teacher for a date, she finally told him to write her a note suggesting a time and place to meet. Well, she didn't show up, and the following day he began to reprimand her and hinted that he would not recommend her for tenure. Well, he got the shock of his life when she told him that she had given his note to her grandmother who worked for an influential member of the Board of Education. Her point made, he put her in for tenure in a timely fashion.

Chapter 17

Graduate School

AFTER MY HUSBAND DIED, there was a time when I was so depressed that I wasn't sure what direction my life was going to take. As a young widow, I considered getting drunk daily, flirting with a series of men, and other ignoble ventures. In the end, I decided what I really wanted to do was teach. The opportunity presented itself to go to graduate school to become more proficient in my profession.

Over a period of time, I would leave young George with mama and go off for a course or a semester to Boston University and even a summer at the University of Hawaii. By immersing myself in my studies, I believed I saved my soul and became a stronger person to care for my family.

When George was ten, I decided that I wanted to go to the University of Indiana, which was offering a summer program dealing with demonstration schools for young children. Taking such a course, I figured, would be good for both my son and me. George, hearing I was going to Indiana, said, "Mama, don't leave me, anymore." Determined not to, I decided that he would accompany me to the university and forwarded my application.

In due time, I was accepted, and off we went by bus and train to Indiana. On arrival, I registered and also signed up George as children of the graduate students were needed to participate in the program. I said nothing about his race on his form, and my instructor did not make a point of it when I met with him to discuss the program. Remember, though, that it was about 1954, when integration was becoming the law of the land, but many people—even in Indiana—opposed it.

Shortly after arriving for class, I overheard several classmates noting that there was a black boy in the demonstration school. One of them said, "I'll only believe it when I see it. His mother or father must be white and whichever registered him sight unseen."

On hearing that remark, I spoke right up, saying, "I'm his mother, and I registered him. He looks like both his mother and his father."

Without any hesitation, the woman snapped back, "How did you have the nerve to register him in this program? How could you do that to your child? He's the only black in the class."

How could I explain to her that George had no awareness of prejudice and would never think for a moment that he was out of place or unwanted in the class. He had been taught to respect the good in all people and to shun evil in all forms and colors of folks. He grew up witnessing that I had many friends that were both black and white. He had been told about Paine College, which I attended and which had never forced segregation on its faculty or student body.

I remembered again about when I was a child, and we lived among poor black and white farmers, and everybody grew cotton and helped each other when possible to pick it. Papa had promised a white neighbor that his children would help the farmer with his cotton the next day. Unbeknownst to him, mama overheard the conversation.

The next morning, mama got up early to prepare breakfast and make up our lunches before waking us. When papa went out to feed the mules, mama opened the front door and told us to hightail it to school.

"You get out of here. Run all the way until you cross the creek. When you're out of Papa's sight, you can walk on to the schoolhouse. You will get an education."

Papa was truly upset when he found out that mama had sent us off to school. Mama, though, would have none of it. "Do you think for a moment that our children are going be picking his cotton while his children go to school?"

One day at the university, George did not come out at his usual time. I went into Mr. Davis' classroom and found him sweeping the floor with an oversized broom and another little lad with red hair and freckles picking up strewn paper. The teacher was surprised to see me and seemed a bit embarrassed.

"Mrs. Crawford," he said, " I did not ask your son to sweep the floor. You see, every day after class, I ask for volunteers to clean up and most of the boys rush out without offering to lend a hand. George and his friend, Tim, always volunteer for this task. I am very grateful to them both."

I pointed out to Mr. Davis that George had been raised "to clean up before he leaves his room."

My response and attitude put Mr. Davis at ease, and he showed me the two boys' class work. He said George and Tim were two of his best students in every way.

On another occasion when I missed George after class, I went to the cafeteria and found him seated at a table with his friend Tim. To my amazement, the two boys were each trying to eat a sirloin steak almost as big as themselves. I learned later that their teacher had bought the steaks for them. I thought their friendship was a wonderful example of how blacks and whites could get along with "nary" a wisp of prejudice.

Since children were not permitted to live on campus, I found a small three-room house for George and me in an unnamed alley in town. Concerned about receiving my mail, I went to the local post office and asked whether I could put up a sign that would give the alley a name. The post office people thought that was a fine idea.

I was quite surprised to see how warm and friendly the neighbors were right from the start. They brought us hot bread on Sunday morning and reminded the ice man to leave us ice daily. They took to watching over George when he went out to play in the neighborhood. Still, for a time they would never come to visit or talk with us but did have a ready smile whenever we passed. I sensed that they felt intimidated by my education because they were poor working people although I never gave it a thought at the time. Later, however, several families began having us by for Saturday supper.

Sadly, this relationship came to an end when a young black woman and man began doing research in the neighborhood for her doctoral thesis. It required a lot of interviews with the young children, and their parents readily agreed until they heard she had criticized the neighborhood children as being too ignorant for her work. To make things worse for us, the rumor mongers said she asked to test my George because she needed to query children with higher IQs and the demonstration school had given her his name.

After her sweep through the neighborhood, there were no more hot rolls on Sunday, and we had to alert the ice man ourselves. The invitations to chitterling suppers also ended. We didn't understand at first what was going on until a little boy told George that he was too stupid to play with my son. George, of course, didn't know what he was talking about, but it occurred to me how foolish and insensitive the young black woman had been in her dealings with these people.

I tried hard thereafter to mend fences, but things never were the same as before. I also determined at that point that a doctoral degree never would mean that much to me. I was glad that the summer program would soon be over, and we could go home. My studies at Indiana University had been spoiled by the damage inflicted by those educators.

In a final effort to make amends, I invited some neighborhood children by to have homemade ice cream. Only a few parents, however, would let their children visit. To those who did come, I told them they could be "what they jolly well pleased"—lawyers, doctors, teachers, anything they set their hearts to be.

I sensed that these children had no role models to inspire them to get an education and move ahead. Their parents only went to the university to work as maids, maintenance people, and janitors. I let them know in no uncertain terms that many doors would be open to them if they became educated and had skills and talents needed by society.

I emphasized that "the doors are opening to you black boys and girls but don't expect anybody to give you anything for nothing. You've got to work for success. Say to yourself, 'Since the doors are opening, I'll work to get through them and be somebody. I'll get it by myself.'"

I hated to think that a limited experience and a blurred view of life would keep them from exploring all the possibilities opened to them. They didn't have to go to college, but it should be their decision—not their parents, some of whom might not understand the importance and the rewards of higher education. It was with that in mind, and the hope that he might go into one of the professions one day that I had enrolled George in the demonstration program.

At the end of the summer, George and I went home to Augusta—again via bus and trains which were then integrated because of the civil right laws originally proposed by President Truman years before. I went back to teaching at the Ursula Collins School. About that time, mama complained of not feeling well and went to Anderson, South Carolina, to live with my sister. It wasn't too long afterward that Lizzie Oglesby Burton died, and the family came together to bury her beside papa in the Norman Grove Cemetery in Elbert County. She had been a loving, concerned, and inspiring mother to all of us. I miss her, still.

Do you believe the dead can talk to you? I truly have to wonder. After mama died, I went to school every day all dressed in black. I was sad all the time and missed her terribly. I wasn't much fun to be around.

Then one night, I had a dream, and I saw mama clad in a long white garment asleep on a beautiful white bed and half covered with a white spread. She opened her eyes and said, "Janie Ruth, look at me. Do I look peaceful and happy?"

When I answered that she did, mama said, "Fine. Then take off that black clothing and begin to be happy, too."

The very next morning, I put aside my black dress and put on a red one and went off to school in a gay mood. Everyone noticed the change in me. My students were especially delighted that I was my old self and complimented me for wearing the bright colored dress.

Chapter 18

Integration

AS THE YEARS ROLLED BY, it seemed like everyone in Georgia was locking horns over the issues of segregation and integration. They steadily grew to become issues of great importance but also assumed the outlines of a fearsome storm on the horizon. Still, we black teachers were convinced that integration would improve both the education of blacks and whites and bring badly needed relief to us, personally.

In the early 60s, teachers were provided booklets and news clippings which spelled out cases where black children had failed compared to white ones. To this day, I can remember walking into my classroom and finding black and white pamphlets containing so-called test scores and other "evidence" to substantiate this claim. Since I was familiar with most of the research they cited, I immediately saw how quotes had been taken out of context or altered to make their argument.

At the time, the authorities also gave us questionnaires to fill out which had nothing to do in any way with teaching. The questions included: "Have you ever been a member of the National Association for the Advancement of

Colored People? Are you a member of it now? Have you ever been a member of a number of other organizations which had no connection to teaching?" Additionally, there were many questions dealing with our family histories that quite frankly were of a personal nature and nobody's business.

In truth, most of the questions were silly, ridiculous. I couldn't believe that anyone would ever bother to read the answers. It was just another form of harassment by diehards who couldn't accept the fact that integration had become a way of life—even in Georgia—and there was nothing they could do about it.

It was also an unwritten law then that if any principal registered a white child in a black school or a black child in a white school, the principal or whoever would automatically be discharged.

I remember that there was a family who never tried to establish their race or color. It was said that a white baby had been found on a black woman's doorstep, and she took the baby and raised it as her own. When the child came of age and noticed that his color was different than his mother's, she explained the situation to him. The little boy loved her very much and vowed never to let race make him hate anyone.

Later, he married a very light-skinned woman, and they had a little girl who came of school age during this trying period. When she sought to register, the teacher sent her to the principal, and he called the superintendent who said her father would have to get a copy of her birth certificate, but the one he got from the hospital failed to name her race.

The principal said the father in that case would have to state his race for the record. The father simply said, "I am what you see." By this time, the affair had been picked up by the media, and his remark was published in the local newspapers.

When the white officials continued to press him for his race, the father decided enough was enough. He said he would not have his daughter harassed any further on the subject. He ceased his attempt to enroll her in public school and put her in a private school, instead.

Later when his mother died, white friends of his were surprised to see that the deceased was a black woman. But the man had the love and courage to remain faithful to the black woman and her family who had raised him. While he undoubtedly could have blended easily into the white world, he held fast to his roots in the black one.

You have to remember that during the late 50s, before integration came into effect, there were no blacks on the Richmond County Board of Education. It was really rough to be a black teacher because we had no one to speak for us before the board.

The principal of the school had all the authority. What he said was law. If you couldn't get along with him, you had to go find another principal who hopefully would hire you. Even if you were hired elsewhere, the superintendent and the principal both had to approve the transfer, and if either one or both had it in for you, your chances of being hired at another school were slim at best. You might say it was like jumping out of the hot skillet into the fire.

The white superintendents made it very apparent that they had little or no respect for the black teachers. They tended to ignore black teacher problems and let the principals tend to them.

Once I remember that we were told to raise a specific amount of money by seeking contributions from our students. Fail to do so, and you would be sent to the superintendent for a tongue-lashing. To raise the sum, my students and I tried to sell peanuts, popcorn, and other items but still failed to come up to our assigned goal. Most of the children themselves were poor and couldn't make any contribution.

Shortly, I was ordered to report to the superintendent's

office. When I entered his office, he took off his shoes and propped his feet on the desk and said, "What are you here for?"

I tried to explain how poor my children were and how it wasn't possible for us to raise the money requested. In turn, he told me to go back out there and do what the principal had asked you to do. I asked him what was wrong, why didn't he understand that we didn't have the necessary resources to raise the sum? He told me that if I didn't meet my goal, he personally would deal with the principal for his failure.

Later, this same superintendent had to find a replacement for a French teacher who had taken maternity leave. He hired a substitute teacher who had a master's degree in foreign languages and was the daughter of a college professor. She turned out to be an excellent teacher, and the students liked and respected her very much.

All went well until the principal criticized her for wearing short skirts. She was dispatched forthwith to the superintendent who ordered her to lower the hems of her skirts or lose her job. She went back to her classroom, said good-bye to her pupils, and went fishing. She was replaced by a substitute teacher who didn't even know French.

The superintendent and the principal had the knack of taking some ridiculous incident and blowing it out of all proportion. Some of these matters were silly, others often tragic. No matter, we went on teaching, we needed the money, and the children needed us. There was always this bond between the teacher and her students.

Later on, we got to elect our first black member of the Board of Education, W. C. Ervin. He was a dynamic and highly educated gentleman who was very people-oriented. For the first time, I felt that I had someone I could talk to about school problems and be heard with respect and concern.

Mr. Ervin made a big difference to us black teachers because of the way he looked out for us and showed how genuinely interested he was in advancing our goals. Right off the bat, he told the Board of Education that black teachers should receive the same pay as white teachers. Then white teachers were being paid more just because they were white even though in many cases the black teachers held higher degrees.

It was ridiculous. On one hand, the whites would say we were highly certified but still not qualified for equal pay. At the same time, they would not allow blacks to enroll in any master's degree programs in Georgia, particularly at the state university. But they would pay for us to attend graduate schools and programs outside of the state. That's how I got to take graduate programs at Boston University and Indiana. I especially liked taking courses at B.U. because I got to see members of my family living in the Boston area. Yet, it was a stupid way to deal with us because it cost the Georgia taxpayers far more for us to go out of state rather than go within the state.

During his four-year term, Mr. Ervin made a big difference in our work lives. Unfortunately, he was not reelected to a second term. To keep a black from winning the post again, the white establishment changed the wards assigned to his district, redrew voting lines, and pulled a few other tricks to ensure a white plurality. In time, though, a black would win the post again, and our aspirations for equal pay with white teachers would be realized.

Through it all, we understood that we could neither wallow in anger nor be consumed by hate for our oppressors. As for myself, my sentiment was biblical: "Lord, forgive them for they know not what they do." I tried to think positively and to concentrate as firmly as ever on teaching as if the woods were on fire.

Another time, we had a special meeting of the local teachers association to deal with the issue of integration, and the white leader requested a vote on the issue even though it had become law. Before any of the black teachers even had a chance to vote, he announced the results—

the majority of the white teachers, of course, had voted against integration.

We felt terribly betrayed and angry. Several of the black teachers questioned the procedure, but the white leader said the vote was binding. He insisted that we had been too slow in getting in our votes.

The key facet of integration initially called for white teachers to teach black children and black teachers to teach white kids. Later, the two races would be mixed in classrooms. I was still at the Ursula Collins school but sort of cut my ties to it when I refused to sign a paper from the school board stating that I would not teach white children.

The principal was up in arms when another teacher and I said we would and could teach white children if the opportunity arose. He called a faculty meeting to further humiliate us by saying, "Two teachers have informed me that they could and would teach white children and in a white school. I want to assure them, though, that they will not be wanted in other schools."

Initially, only light-skinned teachers were selected to teach at all white schools. This ploy didn't work out because they were not always the best teachers. In time, the officials said they only wanted the best black teachers at white schools.

Chapter 19

Black and White

I WAS STILL AT URSULA COLLINS but not for long. A young and inexperienced black teacher was notified that she was being transferred to teach at the white school in one of the poorest and roughest white areas of the city. The young lady had gotten into a sticky situation earlier with a supervisor, and this was his way of seeking revenge.

I heard about it and volunteered in her stead. I felt that I was an experienced well-trained teacher who could handle the white students far more readily than she. I won't say I wasn't looking toward the assignment without a bit of trepidation because I was. In effect, I was given a bunch of lemons and found a way to make lemonade.

The principal at the white school had a record of dislike for blacks, but I found out later that this was not altogether true. Basically, he just disliked lazy and incompetent teachers and assumed you were one until you proved otherwise. In our very first interview, he wanted to know what I thought about "this integration."

I told him that as a civics teacher working in a democratic society I believed in obeying the law of the land.

He next asked how I felt about teaching white children. I said, "Just remove the word white, and I can answer your question. I see children as children. Not as black or white. Children are not a problem to teach. The problem is created by parents and our society."

Without comment, he asked, "What do you think about whites and blacks socializing?"

"Well, do you mean would I want to visit your home or invite you to mine? It's really not pertinent in my case as I already have friends and associates of both races. I don't need integration to dictate to me or to force anyone to accept some undesirable character as a friend."

As black teachers moved into white schools, they got only the level of respect they insisted upon. The black cooks and maids always ate in the kitchen, and they were prompted to invite the new black teachers to join them, while the white teachers ate in the lunchroom. I wouldn't have any of that and, on the very first day, walked into the lunchroom and sat at the center of the most prominent table.

At first, the white teachers ignored me, taking seats at tables around mine. No one sat at my table until Mrs. Williams, a white woman, entered and sat down right beside me. She smiled and introduced herself, and we engaged in a lovely conversation about our hobbies and teaching.

In time, I became very friendly with many of the teachers and ate lunch with them every day in the lunchroom. Some of them became such good friends that they would rush to get a seat beside me. As we felt more comfortable together, we talked also about the school and the students.

Seeing how I was faring, most of the black teachers stopped bringing their lunch and eating it in the kitchen and began taking seats in the lunchroom. We soon began to be treated as "real" teachers and to earn compliments from the parents. Since most of us came from an impoverished background, we could relate quite easily and honestly with our poor white children. The children loved the interaction of helping us make our own teaching tools and looked forward to maintaining the bulletin board and other class projects.

Over the next two years, the principal and I established an excellent working relationship and became good friends. Understand though that all was not rosy at times. One day, a student came to me and said, "I know I won't learn anything this year because we can't understand you folks."

My first reaction was to show anger, but I quickly extinguished that instinct and instead spoke to the young girl briefly in French and then German. "Those are two foreign languages which I don't expect you to understand."

Then I asked her, "Do you speak English at home?" She replied in the affirmative and I said, "Well, I speak English, too, so I'm sure you won't have any problem learning this year in my class. Just make sure you tell your parents that we all speak English here and that you will learn."

On another occasion, a student brought back his corrected paper and claimed that I didn't know how to add. He said his cousin, a college student, had graded his paper and said that I had cheated him out of two points. The college student then told his friends that blacks didn't know how to add.

I told the student that he had a very smart cousin and brought him around to my side of the desk and went over his paper line by line with him. I then showed him my grading chart and explained how it, in effect, did the grading for me so that everybody got the mark they had earned. We went over his paper, and I showed him how I had charted the grade his cousin disputed.

Because I took a personal interest in his concern, we became quite good friends, and I always let him grade his papers. Sometimes, I even let him grade other students' papers although I'd check his math. He was another poor child who only needed someone to take a personal interest in him as well as help and understand his needs.

Then there was the child who told me he always had made A's in spelling, and I had given him a C. He said his mama would be coming to see me about this mark, and she soon did. She argued that she worked diligently with her son on his spelling. "I know he should get an A," she said, "because I call out 10 words every night until he can spell each one correctly."

The woman was wearing a white uniform with a registered nurse's pin attached. "Mam," I said, "I see that you are a registered nurse, and I would never attempt to second guess you on how to care for your patients. Your pin tells me that you are an obviously well-trained professional. Now we teachers don't wear pins, but I can assure you that I am a certified teacher which you can check with my permission at the Board of Education. If you do, you can also ask them to let you read my resume."

With my teaching credentials established in her mind, I went on to discuss her child and my method of teaching spelling. "Here is the speller I use. I would be a poor teacher just to call out words and have the children memorize their spelling. That way is not real teaching. Certainly, if I call all the words in order, your child could memorize them and spell them correctly."

I added that I didn't teach that way, explaining that I called words in any order. I also had the pupils use the words in sentences so they could understand their meaning. I further encouraged them to find antonyms and synonyms of the words.

I repeated that if she really wanted her child to be a good speller, she should stop calling out the words in order. I suggested that she help her son more by doing the numerous related exercises with him. I took up the textbook, and together we did the exercises in one chapter.

The white mother had come to see me in a very defiant mood, probably thinking a black teacher was not competent to teach her son. She left a very grateful woman after thanking me for showing such interest in her child. At Christmas, she sent me a beautiful note, one that was almost apologetic, along with a gift.

When the classrooms became slowly integrated, we had disciplinary problems with both white and black students. Unfortunately, as a result of integration, black children picked up all the white kids' ugly habits and vice versa. Talk about double jeopardy. We had doubly bad problems in conduct. An experienced teacher, though, found ways to work through them.

Then another time, a black mother came to school to confront me and, as she said, "To get you told." I listened as she raged on about black teachers punishing black children and letting the whites off. She charged that her son told her I was "easier on whites than blacks."

In response, I asked her whether she had ever read Dr. Bond's book about the plus factor for blacks. When she answered in the negative, I asked whether her son had ever claimed that I had punished him when he wasn't guilty, and again she answered in the negative.

"You listen," I said, "he's taking off after the banker's son who does give me trouble, but his father will have a job waiting for his son when he graduates. He won't have one waiting for your son. Instead, your son will be dependent upon me for a recommendation. As a result, your son has to be better able to compete with all races, colors, and creeds. It's not quite fair, but it's reality, and I'm trying to prepare him for it."

I told the mother that her son's future was also in her hands. "You have to decide whether you want him to just get by and probably land on welfare or to come to grips with himself and prepare to be the best he can be."

She was quiet and thoughtful for a few moments. Then she nodded her head and smiled thinly. "Yes, Mam, I can see your point. I'd just never thought of it that way."

Early on there were many teachers who just weren't

ready for the demands of integration. They included both black and white teachers.

One particular white teacher was forever dismissing a black girl from her class to wait in the hallway until the class was over. Whenever I went out to the lady's room, I'd see this big, husky, but attractive girl hanging about the steps grinning to herself or acting silly in some way. It soon occurred to me that she and her teacher had a problem. I knew I couldn't interfere with the teacher, but I could try to help the girl.

"Hi, Jane," I said, "why do I see you standing out here in the hall each day?"

Jane replied, "That white teacher just doesn't like me. If I open my mouth at all, she sends me out here to wait until class is over."

"Well," I said, "you can't learn anything waiting out here. Tell you what—the next time she sends you out, bring your English book with you."

Sure enough, the next day, there was Jane out in the hallway with her book. I told her to read the story about "The King's Jester," and then we'd talk about it at recess.

When we met she said, "I understand what you are trying to tell me now. If you are going to be a fool, get paid for it."

We laughed together. I told her when she was permitted back in class to remember the story's message and to stop being the class clown. I reminded her that even if the teacher ignored her, she could learn just by listening to the teacher instructing another pupil.

Thereafter, I never saw her hanging about the hallway. Her teacher did ask me what I had said to Jane, and I said, "She talked and I listened. I talked and she listened."

The poor white children in the school were constantly referred to by white teachers and students as poor white trash. I never used the term, but I heard it in my classroom.

Oftentimes, I would say to a child, "I knew you were

white. I knew you were poor..."

The child would interrupt and finish, "but you didn't know we were poor white trash."

I'd say in reply that God had made each child, and he didn't make trash.

Chapter 20

The Augusta Riot

ONE OF MY ASSOCIATES was a young white teacher, a very sincere and dedicated woman. Three of our pupils, a sister and two brothers, had a very poor attendance record, and when they did come to school, it was obvious they were very poor and hungry. Despite it all, they were smart.

My teacher friend and I thought it would be a good idea to visit their parents and find out what could be done to encourage them to attend class on a regular basis. It was the law, after all. However, the children told us no one was allowed on their property—that their father would shoot any trespassers. Finally, we were able to get their mother to come to the school.

She told us that her husband was a foreign soldier who had come to Fort Gordon for special training. Twice divorced and with the trio of kids, she had married him although he despised children. He even had asked her to get rid of them, somehow, but she had prevailed upon him to let them stay. We got her to give us permission to visit sometime when he was out in the field on maneuvers.

The day came, and we drove out in my friend's car. We

had to go down a winding dirt road, through a wooded lot, and over a small bridge to a ramshackled house. The mother informed us that her husband didn't permit the children to live in the house. She directed us to drive on about a quarter of a mile until we saw a brush arbor.

There, to our horror, we found the children had made a crude brush hut to live and sleep in. They were naked except for rags wrapped around their private parts. They told us that they were only fed twice a week at the house, and the rest of the time, they had to forage for berries or whatever they could get off the land. One boy said his little sister often ate dirt to dull her hunger pangs.

We were in a real quandary as to what to do to help the children. The mother had made us promise beforehand not to say anything to the authorities or otherwise her husband would beat her and force her to get rid of the children. No matter, we knew we had to help them, somehow. I argued that I had dealt many times with problems of poor blacks, and she should handle this one because it involved poor white children.

In the end, we decided to think it over some more. I said, "Let's not tell each other what we will do. I know one of us will do something to bring this matter to the attention of the school officials."

A brief while later, the children withdrew from school because their father was transferred to another fort. When they left, I couldn't get them out of my heart. Our children are such precious assets and so many times we waste them. One thing, though, I was confident about: Those children were smart. They were survivors. They would make it.

Most people in the South loved President John F. Kennedy. He was so bright and witty and handsome, but mostly because he had fought hard for civil rights and had died while trying to implement them. He introduced so many changes in federal programs that were helpful to blacks.

I was especially fond of him and often visited Boston while he was president. Several times, I went to Cape Cod to see Hyannis Port, the summer home of the Kennedy clan. In those days, there was constant talk, gossip, and speculation about Jackie and Caroline and the new baby that was due. He would be little John-John.

On November 22, 1963, about 1:30 p.m., I was in the classroom with 62 students. Can you imagine trying to teach that many at once? Suddenly, the principal, in a loud painful voice, announced over the loudspeaker, "John F. Kennedy, the President, has been shot in Dallas."

The children and I literally froze in place. We were stunned as though struck by a lightning bolt. We cried and prayed and hoped for news of his recovery. Instead, the news said that officials had sent for a priest. Our hearts fell because we recognized then there was no hope.

The classroom became deathly silent. I was speechless. I simply put down my head and murmured several prayers for the repose of his soul.

Dr. Martin Luther King Jr. was another great hero of my people. I had heard him speak several times. One time, when he was in Augusta to speak in the Tabernacle Baptist Church, I called to him as he was walking up the steps with his entourage: "Oh, Martin, you're so handsome. I would just like to kiss you."

Well, I nearly died when he came right over to me and knelt down and said, "Go ahead, kiss me." And I did, right on the cheek.

I sort of got to know him because of his visits to Augusta, and I knew his father, too. In fact, I had dinner with him once.

Little did I know that five years later on April 4th at seven p.m., Martin Luther King would be fatally shot when he stepped out onto the balcony of the Lorraine Motel in Memphis. Fortunately for me, I was not in the classroom with my students on that sad occasion and was able to grieve in privacy. The next day, though, I had to deal with the students' shock and grief over his loss.

It was a terrible tragedy for all of us, and his memory will live forever in the hearts of humanity. Each year since then, we celebrate his birthday, January 15th, as a national holiday in all but a few states.

I also had the privilege in my lifetime to meet Thurgood Marshall, who was a Supreme Court justice. I've always considered it a rewarding experience to have conversed with Judge Marshall on several occasions.

Throughout the country during the late 60s and early 70s, there was much division among the people, mostly over the war in Vietnam and civil rights issues. It seemed that there was always a demonstration or a rally or a sit-down strike or a riot occurring in some section of the country. A series of them erupted when Martin Luther King was assassinated—particularly in Los Angeles, New York, and Miami.

Two years later in May, 1970, there was a tragic riot in Augusta. A mob of black youths converged on the Municipal Building after a teenage black boy was beaten to death by two other black inmates in the Richmond County Jail. The crowd wanted to know why jail officers hadn't prevented the beating and generally to protest jail conditions.

The authorities failed to "cool down" the mob which then decided to hold a peaceful protest march. It got out of hand when a Black Panther member allegedly tore down and burned a Georgia state flag and tried to lower an American flag. Law officers intervened, and the riot was under way.

It was a terrible time, and before it was over, six persons were shot to death—all black men—scores injured and property loss was well over a million dollars. A dusk-to-dawn curfew was imposed, and 2,000 National Guard soldiers were ordered into the city by the governor.

Firemen were hampered in battling more than 30 blazes by sniper fire.

It was a horrible scary time for all of us—especially in the black community with the curfew and the troops stationed in the city for a week. I felt despair and sadness for the loss of lives and the injured and for so much destruction. The black neighborhoods suffered badly with most of the destruction concentrated in a 130-square block area of the city.

Most of the time, I was very uneasy and angry. I was always tense and tired. I could not sleep at night because the National Guard tanks were constantly clanking up and down my street. It was impossible even to get a nap after school. Those tanks were out there 24 hours a day. Worst of all, they had the turrets swung around so the big guns were pointed right at my house when they went by.

I was also very upset when it became apparent that school officials were keeping a close eye on all the black teachers. A member of the Board of Education even inquired as to what, if any, role I played during the riot and its aftermath. I was furious that he would even ask me such a question as though I was an instigator of some sort. It showed me how close a check they were keeping on us.

No traffic was permitted on my 15th Street day or night without permission. I had to get a permit to drive to school each day. I could only get off and onto my street by showing the permit at the military road blocks.

Many motorists were stoned in the vicinity of my house in retaliation for the stoning of black cars downtown. In my mind, there was no doubt that it was a racial conflict. In many instances, though, both whites and blacks assisted each other and prevented further deaths and injuries.

One day during that dreadful period, a mentally deranged white woman came onto the school grounds at lunchtime and claimed that a crowd of black folks had burned down a store and were on their way to our school.

The principal immediately had all the children sent inside to their classrooms and came by to talk to me.

I told him that I didn't believe the woman's report. "I know what's going on in the black community just like you know what's going on in the white community. I can tell you that no such march is planned on our school."

When he left reassured, I told my pupils that no one was going to hurt them. I would stand in the doorway if any crowd approached. Fortunately, as I had noted, none ever did.

A little while later, a white student told me that many of the students' fathers were taking turns sleeping in a large warehouse located nearby. She told me that they were all armed and ready to act if any blacks took it upon themselves to try and harm us.

"Here is the phone number where they can be reached. Mama told me to give the number only to our friends."

I thanked the student but said I didn't believe I would need to call the number.

My fear escalated when my younger sister, Costella, telephoned from Boston to say that her son, John Laymon, was on his way to Augusta. He was one of ten volunteer law students from Howard University coming to the city to help bridge the gap between the black and white communities. John and the other students would be working closely with the Augusta Police Department to determine ways to cool down the hostility in both camps. When possible, I let John use my car to get about.

Leaders of the black community were already holding a series of meetings with city and county authorities to discuss many grievances. By the fourth day, a six-part agreement was approved to ease racial tensions. Some 500 soldiers left Augusta that evening, and after a quiet weekend, the remaining 1,500 departed on Monday.

Mayor Millard Beckum, a white man, told the press that he hoped, "we've reached the point where we can talk out our problems. I'm hoping that cool heads and minds prevail."

I said, "Amen," to that.

It's been a long time since those riot days, and I have to say we've made some progress in improving race relations, but we haven't made enough. Laws giving blacks equal rights are fine, but you can't change what's in a man's heart. If Martin Luther King were alive today, I think he'd have to map an entirely new strategy for dealing with civil rights.

Too many blacks and whites who want to help in the struggle are afraid. It's not much different than in old Gene Talmadge's time. They think they'll lose the vote, or they'll lose a friend if they take visible action. So they keep a low profile.

I know how it is because I had many friends, black and white, at the time of the riot, but just then you stayed with your own. There were times and places you just didn't want to be seen together.

One of my dearest white friends was President E. Clayton Calhoun of Paine College, to whom I had just presented a check a few weeks earlier from the Augusta Chapter of the National Association of College Women.

He was kind enough to say, "Mrs. Crawford, you know how badly Paine College needs money, but I need your friendship and support even more."

I wondered whether we could have met in such a wonderful setting during that horrific week in Augusta.

We still have two different worlds. A black one and a white one. But today you can cross over and mix in both. The many changes in the law have brought that situation about.

Just recently, I was at a black tie dinner of the Presidential Club of Paine College, which was hosted by President Scott at the Pinnacle Club, a most sophisticated and prestigious setting in Augusta. The dinner was his way of saying thank you to the club members who had demonstrated their support of the college during the past year. Most of the attendees were black although there were a few white friends present.

Just across the hall, an important group of whites were also holding their own dinner. As it turned out, both affairs broke up at the same time, and we all began filing out to take the elevators to the ground floor. You should've seen their faces when they suddenly realized they were mixing with these very well-dressed blacks.

I don't know how they signaled each other as not a word was spoken. It must be inbred or whatever, but in a flash, the majority of them turned away and headed for this large service elevator. A few white couples in front hadn't picked up on the fact that a black contingent was also waiting and stepped onto the elevator. When they turned and saw who was following in their tracks, they acted like a snake who had gotten loose in the house and slithered around us to escape our presence.

I found it very amusing. We were dressed to the nines, tuxes and gowns, college graduates with respectable careers in our chosen professions. I just looked at them as they oozed by us and smiled.

So you can see even today that there's a standoff attitude that's going to take a long time to go away. But my philosophy is that I don't want to be with anybody who does not want to be with me. You're the one with a problem, not me. No one is better than me, and nobody is lower. I'm a very independent woman. That's the way I was raised. One thing I don't have is an inferiority complex. I accept everybody and hope others feel that way about me.

Chapter 21

Final Days

OVERALL, THOSE YEARS WHEN INTEGRATION was going into effect were rewarding in many ways. Mostly because teachers had a sense that parents had come around to genuinely appreciate them for the help they were giving to their children. Parents noted again and again that teachers had stepped in to provide a helping hand when parents weren't available to do so.

But woven into the fabric of helping hands and good deeds were myriad threads of disappointment and sorrow. One white child came up to me in the schoolyard to whisper in my ear that her mother was a prostitute at a major hotel and wanted her to follow in her footsteps when she turned 16. She went on to say how abhorrent the whole idea was to her since she despised older men.

I emphasized that she didn't have to do that type of work no matter what her mother said. I asked her why she was talking to me about it. She said because I was black and did not know her mother or her white friends. She added that her mother would kill her if she found out that she had talked to anyone about her work.

I did talk to her mother, but, of course, I never said a

word about what her daughter had told me. Rather, I stressed the need for her to encourage her daughter to remain in school and get a good education. I pointedly observed that every mother "wants her children to do better than she did." I must've had some effect on the woman because the girl remained in school when she turned 16 and later graduated with her class. She obviously had concluded that her original advice to her daughter was wrong.

Many of my pupils came from military families at Fort Gordon, and a lot of them were very capable of learning while others had trouble grasping lessons. But it was surprising to me how many of them also had learned so much by traveling from post to post with their families.

One time, I was teaching about the Boston Tea Party, and something came up about the swan boats in the Public Garden, which led to a discussion generally about swans. I remarked how the white swan was so beautiful and graceful, and a little girl popped up that "they aren't so beautiful as the black swan."

Thinking she was being smart, I said, "There is no such thing as a black swan." She shook her head in disagreement. So I said, "I'll believe it when I see a photograph of one. If you have one, please show it to me."

Well, to my surprise, the very next day the girl came to class with several photos of black swans. The photos were taken in Alaska, where her family had been stationed and often saw black swans. Of course, I apologized, reminding myself again that many of these children had different experiences than mine to draw upon.

Another time I made the sweeping remark that the guards do not let visitors take photographs at the Pearl Harbor memorial battle site. As soon as I finished, a little hand went up, and a boy informed me that his family had been stationed at Pearl Harbor and had many photographs of the area. His name was John, and the next day he came to school to share his Pearl Harbor photographs with the class.

I continued to notice during this time that white teachers had a real problem teaching white children of impoverished families. They also had a problem about taking these children on field trips. They just didn't want to be seen with them.

As one white teacher said to me, "It's okay for you because you're black, but some people might think these are my own children. I'd be terribly embarrassed."

Many times, I'd fill in for these teachers and take their classes on the field trips. We'd go off to museums and city hall to visit the mayor, to chat with bankers, and sit in courtrooms to watch the proceedings. The students loved it since they got out of classroom work and gained new experiences. I found them to be well behaved, curious and interested, and we usually had a grand time.

Over a period of time, I noticed that the white principal seemed suspicious of my teaching methods although I was only trying to teach as always as if the woods were on fire. I suspected that he couldn't understand how a black teacher got along so well with so many white children and seemed to be so well regarded by them. He didn't seem to realize that all I was doing was teaching, and the children were learning.

Anyway, I got so irked with his constant snooping and peeking at the classroom window that I wrote two letters of resignation, one to him and one to the Board of Education. I personally delivered his copy and announced that I was resigning immediately.

He turned red and appeared to be distressed and asked me why. "You are a fine teacher. You are respected by the children. They are much better behaved since you took over. You know three other teachers failed to bring them under control."

He added that I couldn't leave. What could the children possibly have done to make me resign?

I noted that the children weren't the problem, he was

the problem. "I'm tired of you always spying on me and checking up on me. I see you peeking into my room from the hallway window. I do not appreciate being under your constant surveillance."

A flash of understanding crossed his features. "Oh, Mrs. Crawford, please tear up that letter," he said referring to the copy for the Board of Education. At the same time, he tore up the copy I had given him without even reading it.

He said, "I can't believe how those children have changed since you took over the class. You know, any school must have order to teach properly, and you have helped immensely in making that possible. It's important, too, that we keep the parents happy, and you have been a big help in that department. Many of them have told me how happy they are that their children have a teacher who cares about them and teaches them so many things."

He closed by saying that "I need you. I have much to learn from you."

Pleased with his kind words, I smiled and said, "Wouldn't it be much easier for you to just come into the class and sit and listen?"

He expressed the view that he could learn more about the reaction between teacher and pupils when they were unaware that he was viewing them. He noted that I only became aware of him because I had the habit of walking about my classroom while teaching. Anyway, we had a very thorough conversation and cleared the air and soon became good friends.

Later, when the principal was transferred to another school, he requested that I accompany him. I was torn about going to this bigger school nearer to my home or staying at the former school where there was still so much to do. Finally, just two weeks before the opening of school, I agreed to the transfer although I would begin the school year with mixed emotions.

At the new school, the student body was a mixture of

mostly white middle class kids and poor black pupils. It was a challenging setup, but I looked forward to this new experience. Once again, numerous remnants of segregation lurked throughout the school. Black teachers chose to remain segregated from their white counterparts their breaks and at lunchtime. There, submitting to this self-imposed humility, they drank coffee and gossiped about the white teachers and their students.

Well, I would have none of that. I had fought that battle before and wasn't about to take a single step backward in the gains we had made. From day one, I ate my lunch with the white teachers and not an eyebrow was raised, and I also took all my breaks in the lounge set aside for that purpose with my white colleagues. You can only be humiliated if you permit yourself to be. The black teachers got the message and soon would join me in enjoying what they were due.

Shortly, I became friendly with many of the white teachers. I remember several of them had the habit of asking about my problem child, "Is that a black child?" I always replied, "He is only a child who needs help to learn."

Another teacher said, "Mrs. Crawford, you come to the lounge daily and talk about your pupils, but you never specify whether they are black or white."

To her I responded, "No, I don't. To do otherwise would point to some prejudice. To me, color of a child's skin doesn't matter. I'm paid only to help each and every child to the best of my ability and in a fair and equitable way."

Some years later, I met this teacher, and she introduced me to her fiance as a woman who spoke her mind without jeopardizing any friendships.

I heard later that I was the subject of conversation at a gathering of black teachers in their old lounge. One of them said, "I think she's just the principal's spy." A teacher, however, who knew me well didn't let that remark go by without comment.

"Never!" she said. "I know her. She's no spy for anyone. She just wants to know what's going on so she can make intelligent decisions based on facts."

Soon afterward, I was invited to meet with some of these black teachers, and they asked me why I was in such a hurry to join the white teachers in the school lounge. For one thing, I said, that was where all the school notices first were posted, and it was also an excellent resource for up-to-date information.

At the same time, if black teachers or children are discussed, I'm at least one black teacher who is there to provide the white teachers with the true facts and to emphasize that we are here to help all the children.

Even after that, though, the conversation would cease at times when I walked into their lounge. I thought about the reason for this for a while and then walked into the lounge one day and simply noted: "My son is an oceanographer and travels all over the world, and he says you can always talk about wine, women, and the weather without stepping on anyone's toes. Wine probably isn't something we'd want to talk about in school. We're all women so perhaps we wouldn't want to talk about ourselves. Since it's a beautiful day, maybe we can stick to the weather."

The teachers either smiled or laughed. I had broken the ice and became one of the group.

I saw many incidents in the schoolyard at recess and overheard many words that I could've reported to the principal but didn't. Children would get into silly little name-calling fights and tease one another. I would mostly ignore them, believing that the children would work out their differences among themselves without adult interference.

One time, a child came up to me and said that her mother had warned her that I better not put a hand on her. Since she was a member of my class, I replied that if she were to stay in my class, she'd have to get use to some touching. I believed in patting a child for a job well done and in poking gently any child who was too loud or out of order.

To my surprise, her mother came rushing up to the school the next day, and I was summoned to the principal's office.

He told me that I did not have permission to whip any child. I informed them both that I didn't need permission because I had never whipped any child and had no intention of ever doing so.

Taken aback, the principal inquired, "Mrs. Crawford, how do you keep order then?"

"If I ever had to whip a child and went to jail, believe me the parents would come and get me out because they'd know their child got what he deserved," I said.

I then explained what I meant by touching a child—especially when a child had done well—and I had patted him or her on the shoulder. I then suggested that the principal have the woman's child transferred to another classroom. I would take the worst child from that room in exchange. My suggestion was acted upon.

A few days later, though, the mother came by to tell me that her child was unhappy with the other teacher and missed my class. I wasn't angry. I understood that many white parents had it in their mind that black teachers only wanted to whip white children. It would take time and understanding to rid them of that ridiculous notion.

There were so many incidents of this nature as we went through the integration process that there just isn't space to relate them here.

Today, some 17 years after I retired, the Richmond County schools are still under the supervision of the federal court and full integration has yet to come to pass. About half a dozen schools remain at least 90 per cent black, and another three have 80 per cent or more blacks and minorities. Yet, the school enrollment for the county is about 50-50 black and white. So you can see there's still work to be done before there's an end to court supervision.

Chapter 22

Closing the Books

I DECIDED IN 1977, that I would retire from teaching. It was the year that Jimmy Carter, the earnest young peanut farmer from Plains, became the first American president from Georgia. It was difficult to believe that I had been a teacher for 38 years. I had only fond memories of my first teaching job in the town of Blakely.

Being a teacher had been an enormously rewarding career for me. I like to think that in my chosen career I had touched many lives for the better and had been touched in kind by so many dear folks. At the end of the school year, I was presented with a lovely silver tray at a ceremony that finally convinced me my teaching days were truly over.

Some 17 years after my retirement, I still fully believe that it is imperative that young people get a good education if they are to survive and get ahead in this world. It doesn't necessarily have to be a formal college education, but it must be one that will permit them to cope with the world we live in today.

You've got to be able to listen and understand. If you can't read or write, you can't do much of anything except stoop labor. You can't clean a house because you can't read the labels on the various cleaning liquids and sprays. And you can't cook because you can't read recipes or the labels on the cans and bottles.

It's so sad to see people who can't read an application for work. I have people telling me all the time that they can do a certain job but can't apply because they can't fill out the application. Education is the only way out of the poverty trap.

With my small retirement from the state of Georgia and Social Security, I took a break to decide what I wanted to do with the rest of my life. My son George, after ten years with the U.S. Oceanographic Service, had returned to school to get his degree in dentistry. He was practicing dentistry in Aiken, South Carolina, where he lived with his wife, Delores, and my three precious grandchildren—Christine Ruth, George I. Jr., and Marcus. They're only about half-an-hour's drive away, and we visit quite often. It's very reassuring knowing that these beloved members of my family are so close by.

Not very long after I retired, I undertook a second career—never intending that it would be a full-time one, but that's what it turned out to be. Right across from my house on 15th Street was a trio of dilapidated structures—a one-time orphanage which was forced to close in the early 60s due to lack of funds. They stood on seven acres of land.

One of the buildings was in somewhat fair condition and was used as a satellite welfare office for the distribution of food stamps, and every day I could see the people standing in line for their quota. But at night, I couldn't help noticing that a stream of black youths gathered about it to buy and sell drugs. Later, I saw tents and old mattresses and other debris left over after a series of drug parties.

My heart burned within me as I tried to think of some other use to make of this property. I began to talk to some folks about alternative uses, but nobody seemed interested. It only made me more determined to come up with a solution.

Finally, one day I saw a sign that said the property was to be rezoned for a home for alcoholics. My research showed that the majority of these people were well off and that their families wanted them placed where no one would know them. At one rezoning meeting, I asked what would happen if any of these alcoholics returned to the home after drinking all day. I was informed that they would not be permitted to enter the building which meant they would be roaming around the neighborhood in an inebriated condition and who knows what trouble they would get into late at night.

Thinking of the families around me and their needs, I determined to find a service that would be of more use. Something that had a positive cast to it and would help to upgrade the neighborhood. I called a group of folks together and suggested that the buildings would be better used for a senior citizens community center which could serve the needs of the older residents as well as other neighborhood groups.

It was from this meeting and the seed of an idea that I planted that the Shiloh Comprehensive Community Center grew into a reality. I envisioned the center as a multi-faceted, non-profit, non-sectarian corporation which would serve the social, recreational, educational, nutritional, and health needs of adults and youths in the area.

Oh my, how we struggled that first year to get the center off the ground. There was hardly any money to pay for anything, and a long list of things needed to be done. We had bake sales and rummage sales and beat the bushes constantly to shake free money to pay for the utilities. I had offered my services free of charge—never realizing that an intensive struggle laid ahead to get the project off the ground.

Some 18 years later, I often say that Shiloh was founded on a wing and a prayer. "The wing has cracked, but I'm still praying."

I recruited other volunteers to help implement the center's various service programs. I had to make the center known to the community. I used every means of communication known to me—including speeches to church groups, interviews with the media, and writing innumerable letters to individuals who might be of some help.

Soon we went down to the courthouse and received our charter of incorporation and tax exempt status for the center.

The judge was very complimentary regarding our goals and efforts to date, noting that "this is the first time anyone has come to the court and sought to take this property and make it into something that will be uplifting for the community and its citizens."

He signed the order turning the buildings and land over to Shiloh Comprehensive Community Center. I assured him that we would also make the center available to the people. Shortly, we began working with them on various programs including several tutoring classes.

I must admit that the hardships and struggles we waged to open the center and to keep it afloat took a toll on me. I don't think I ever worked harder at any time in my life—even during the trying and hectic days of segregation and integration. When I taught, I was paid and saved my money for summer school or a vacation—a cruise in the Caribbean or a visit to Hilton Head. In my leadership role at Shiloh, I drew no income and had to forgo many of the old pleasures.

Still, I've never regretted my involvement in Shiloh despite all the hard work, long hours, and unending problems. The many successes make it all worth while. They include Intergenerational Day Camp, where senior citizens and children come together to share dreams and build friendships; the Food Pantry that provides food to individuals and families in need; the annual Thanksgiving Banquet for the able-disabled with volunteers preparing the meals; and the Girl Scouts, which has been meeting and serving area girls since 1978.

It is fair to say that Shiloh is a true community center, reaching all generations and providing a resource of extra stability for the neighborhood.

At a fundraiser on April 20, 1994, Congresswoman Eva McPherson Clayton of North Carolina (though a native of Augusta) said, "I think that Shiloh is one of the best things for the Augusta community...I would like to commend Ruth B. Crawford, the founder of the center, and the volunteers who have caught the spirit of helping others and reaching out..."

She noted that "when you help keep a place open like Shiloh, then it shows that the village still cares about its people."

In my turn, I told the folks in attendance, including Mayor Charles A. DeVaney and Richmond County Commission Chairman Willie Mays, that "the need for funding is an ongoing struggle, one that calls for a general fundraiser every year."

The local newspaper, Augusta *Chronicle,* noted in part that "it's gratifying that black and white Augustans came together to support a worthy endeavor: the Shiloh Community Center. Founder and director Ruth B. Crawford has greatly expanded the center's role of helping young and old to include free lunches, tutoring, support for the Neighborhood Watch program, a limited health program, and other endeavors. More power (and donations) to the center!"

I was so busy at Shiloh for so long that I didn't have time for a boyfriend, least that's what I thought. Finally though, an old friend returned to Augusta, and we began seeing each other. He coaxed me back into the fun of a social life and doing things for pleasure. In his company, I renewed my great love of dancing and often played cards.

If awards were counted as money, I'd be a rich woman. My pleasure and satisfaction in receiving recognition has always been compounded by the acknowledgment from the presenter that I truly deserved the award.

I remember the year 1983, when I received the Jefferson Award from WRDW-TV (Channel 12) for what the station officials termed "dedicated and extraordinary service to mankind."

Only two weeks later, I was asked to meet with Robert Gillespie at University Hospital. I wondered what volunteer job they had in mind and where would I find the time to fit it in. I wondered whether I could muster the courage to turn him down.

Well, he couldn't have been more gracious as we sat in his expansive office and exchanged pleasantries. I finally said, "What is it you want from me? I had to tear myself away from my work to get here."

Mr. Gillepsie smiled in return and said, "Mrs. Crawford, you are a kind and generous woman, diligent and hard-working, and that is why you are here. You have been named Humanitarian of the Year, and your name will be placed on a plaque here in the hospital for all to see. We can't thank you enough for your many contributions to the uplifting of your fellow citizens."

I was so impressed and happy. His words meant more to me than the award. Through the years, my work at the center became known, and the awards were forthcoming in a steady stream, including two from the governor of Georgia. I also had a lovely letter from the White House and had mention of my contributions entered into the Congressional Record in 1991. Mostly, the awards and citations noted that I was the catalyst who changed an abandoned building into a thriving center designed to meet some of the community's deepest needs.

As recently as April, 1994, President Clinton wrote to congratulate me "on being nominated for the 1994 President's Volunteer Action Award." While noting that I was not chosen as a recipient in that year, the president added, "I want to commend your outstanding work that has made such a positive difference in your community."

He noted: "It is through service like yours that we will solve our country's most critical problems and strengthen the bonds that link us as a people. On behalf of all Americans, I thank you for a job well done."

In my heart, I know that any success I have achieved in my life's work goes back to the training, values, and education demanded by my mother and father and from their love and that of my sisters and brothers and my dear son, his wife, and my three grandchildren. I could write about them at length along with my years at Shiloh, but those entries would double the size of this work.

Whatever, I've had a long and fruitful life—one marked by much happiness and scarred somewhat less by sorrow. Still, I plan to make other contributions in my time on earth, God willing.